One Couple's Journey Building a

Montana Cabin...

One Log at a Time

Douglas Reid
and
Nancy Procter

with
Photography by Nancy Procter
and Illustrations by Douglas Reid

Acknowledgments

We'd like to thank the people who read our manuscript and made thoughtful comments on our writing, our spelling and our story.

Thanks to Bill and Kathy Minckler, Jim Procter, Stephanie Salter, Harley Williams and Amy Twiggs. We appreciate your encouragement on our first attempt at authoring a book. We hope others enjoy it at least as much. Unfortunately, any errors and inaccuracies are solely our responsibility, not our reviewers.

We would also like to thank our families. Nancy wishes to express her thanks to her parents, Ed and Sue Procter, who took her on so many car-camping trips and whetted her appetite for adventure. Doug wishes to thank his sisters and their families for all their help and encouragement during the cabin building process.

Privacy Statement

Throughout this book, we have tried to tell our story as accurately as our memories will allow. There are individuals in this story, however, who may not appreciate our honesty. Therefore, some of the names in this book have been changed. Other individuals' names have been altered to protect their privacy and it shouldn't be assumed that those persons were in any way nefarious. Other names have not been altered at all. We hope this policy does not negatively impact our story.

INTRODUCTION

Well, now that he's finished one building,

he'll go write four books about it.

--Frank Lloyd Wright

One Log at a Time is not about how to build a log cabin, although it wouldn't hurt to read it if you are planning on engaging in a similar undertaking. It's more about the journey of a forty-something couple pursuing their dream, our dream. Our goal was to build a simple 1,100 square foot, off-the-grid cabin from scratch in the mountains of southwestern Montana. We struggled, fought heat and cold and snow, had numerous setbacks, and operated on a shoestring. We camped out, on-and-off in a tipi at the cabin-site, and also lived and worked as rangers in Yellowstone Park.

One Log at a Time covers roughly fourteen years, from 1993 to 2007; from the April day we first set foot on our snow-covered land through the day, with horribly mixed emotions, we sold our beloved cabin, and the genesis of our next adventure. Our journey embodies the inspiration, perseverance, sweat, trial-and-error, humor, and satisfaction that comes from doing something on our own. It was a journey that we look back on with great affection, and one that changed our lives.

Table of Contents

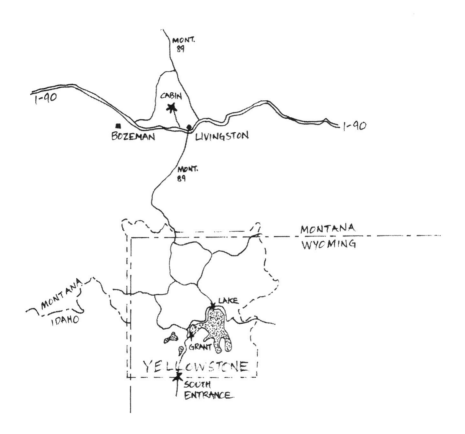

Our Neck of the Woods

Nancy

1

I CAN'T REMEMBER A

HARDER WALK

There it was, there it is, the place where during the best time of our lives friendship had its home and happiness its headquarters.

--Wallace Stegner, Crossing to Safety

Our last visit to the cabin is truly bittersweet. We will be

signing the closing papers in a few days, turning over the ownership to someone else. Based on the few times we saw the new owners, we know that they are salivating with excitement like Pavlov's dog. But will they comprehend, really sense, just how much this right of ownership conveys? As we look around for what we finally realize is "it", the memories flood out. This will be our last night here, our last glass of wine, our last morning coffee, and then, the last goodbye.

We sit quietly, eyes moving around the open area downstairs, from kitchen to living room. We want to take it all in, although it seems ridiculous to think that we will ever forget our time here. Every log, floorboard, stair tread, window buck, trim piece, every single component of this cabin has a memory. Some elicit a smile, some an "I wish I had done that differently", or a "Man, it was cold that day". Our names will no longer be on the deed, but we are the soul of this cabin.

We had arrived back in Montana the evening before, now we settle out on the front porch in our usual positions. The Adirondack chairs lure us, our feet propped on the railing. It is mid-September, 2006, and foliage is turning brilliant colors, temperatures cooling after the sun goes down. Wine glasses sit on the spool table, and we are easily mesmerized by the setting sun on the Absaroka Mountains. It is as though we had never left. The only difference is there is no longer a dog at our feet. Our sidekick of 14 years, O'Malley, had been put to rest a couple of months earlier. It's the first time in nearly thirty years we've been without a dog.

One of the purposes of this trip is to spread some of O'Malley's ashes on the property, around the tipi ring. We've chosen the tipi ring rather than at the cabin site itself, because during the building phase O'Malley toughed it out with us through a few 28 below zero nights. He was the most faithful, most ornery dog on earth and deserves a resting place that is familiar.

Spreading O'Malley's ashes is actually secondary to the real purpose. We've come to clear out. The sale is turn-key, but we agreed to remove items that are personal or those we can't live without. The stop in Montana is on the tail end of a return trip from a wedding in Minnesota, then we will continue on to Utah. We have rented a mini-van for the lengthy trip, a vehicle we assume will be

Douglas Reid and Nancy Procter

well equipped to hold our memories. What we discover is there is no such animal.

The plan is to park the mini-van at the bottom of the county road and transfer into our old 1980 4WD pickup, Rusty, for the last 1 ½ unmaintained miles to the cabin. Rusty, too, is part of the sale. The last stretch of the road, much to our delight, remains just a couple of ruts for most of the year. The rest of the time it is either a mud bog, gumbo, or covered in snow. We figured this helped to keep the "lookie-loos" out and slow down the inevitable development. We aren't the only ones to want our own little piece of paradise.

As we sort through all our possessions in the cabin, we chuckle that most of them are either made from scraps on site or bought at secondhand stores. Yet, it all clicks. It clicks well enough that once the cabin went on the market, it sold within a few months. It is just too charming. But, we know, these things belong with the cabin. They would never fit in the real world. So, we leave way too much behind. After loading a few pieces of sentimental furniture and miscellaneous stuff, the mini-van is bursting at the seams. The transfer of goods comes to an abrupt end, at any rate, when Rusty blows a rod on the last trip back up to the cabin. That pretty much signals the end of Rusty. And Rusty's involvement in the sale. The rest of the memories have to remain.

This morning, we brew our last cup of coffee, wash dishes, lock the doors and windows, and walk down the road. I can't remember a harder walk.

Doug

2

FLAME OUT BEND

When the situation is hopeless, there's nothing to worry about.
--Ed Abbey, Monkey Wrench Gang

I'm heading home after a partial day of work on the cabin on

this early summer day in 1994. It's just me and Cisco and Pancho, our two black lab mutts; Nancy is out of town on business.

Yesterday, when I was up here, I noticed the tipi had a huge rip near the door. Muddy forepaw prints grace the side of the tipi and there's no mistaking them as anything but the work of a black bear. We don't keep any food in the tipi but nonetheless, his investigation left one or two perfect paw prints, a couple of muddy smears and a big rip. I don't think he (she?) went inside, just moseyed around the perimeter and pawed it here and there. Duct tape patches it for now but it's nothing Nancy, the tipi seamstress, can't fix.

When Nancy called home the night before, I told her about the rip and the bear paw prints. It's very exciting and when she tells her colleagues about it they find it intriguing, hearing about a bear sniffing around our tipi. Tonight when she calls I'll have an even more exciting story. It will be about how Flame Out Bend gets its name.

We, Cisco and Pancho and I, head home after a very short morning's work. I've just finished some task or another and I'm going down to Livingston to buy a tool. I'm driving old Brownie, the 1970 GMC 4WD. It's just had the carburetor worked on so that I get more than three miles to the gallon. It's running good now, no complaints. We're crawling up a steep section in the road, in 4WD low range, passing right by a towering old fir tree and about to make a sharp left hairpin turn. As I crank the wheel, I hear a "whoosh" and Brownie comes to an abrupt halt. Smoke starts to pour out from underneath the hood and some is seeping into the cab through the glove box and the heater vents. I pull the parking brake and get out. Smoke keeps simmering from under the hood.

What I should do is get the dogs out of the truck and stand back and wait. Stupidly, what I actually do is get the dogs out of the bed of Brownie and go lift the hood. Bad mistake. The second the additional oxygen reaches the gasoline dripping on the hot engine, it bursts into flame. Now it's too late, all I can do is stand back and wait. The flames begin melting rubber tubes and hoses, smoke billows into the sky. There is absolutely nothing I can do but get farther away from the truck in case it decides to blow. For about five minutes I stand and watch. The windshield cracks and shatters into a million pieces. The seats, foam and and nylon and plastic, smoulder and catch fire. Plastic and foam dashboard padding burns very nicely. So do my coat and leather gloves and the canvas bag they were in. I'm rolling over in my mind the best course of action and I conclude there really is nothing I can do.

The flames reach high enough to begin scorching the fir tree the truck sits right beneath. I decide it's time to quit watching, waiting for something to blow, and get help before I have a forest fire on my hands. I trudge the next 75 yards to the top of the hill and jog down the road to Charlie Story's double-wide trailer about a mile away.

Cisco is ancient at 16. He's on his last legs, and can barely keep up with me, the world's slowest jogger. Pancho's about 12, and he waddles along with me, for once in his life he's faster than Cisco. I knock on Charlie's door. He's an old white-haired gentleman, a retired rancher, about 75 I'd guess, and he answers the door in this t-shirt and socks. I request his help putting out the fire and he goes into action. He shuffles over to get his shoes, a coat and a fire extinguisher. I put the dogs in the back of Charlie's pickup. Cisco is exhausted and can't stay on his feet. Charlie starts up the hill like we're going to a four-alarm fire, which in a sense we are. As we bounce along on the horrible rutted road, I look back at Cisco and Pancho in the bed and they are bouncing a foot in the air each time we hit a major rock or rut.

"Slow down, Charlie," I yell. "If that frickin' trees' on fire, that little fire extinguishers' not gonna do any good at all."

We arrive at the scene in about five minutes. Charlie's truck suspension will never be the same. Brownie is literally toast. The engine compartment and cab are still smouldering so we spray them down with the fire extinguisher. The seats are nothing but coils of wire. The steering wheel is a circle of blackened steel and the naugahyde steering wheel cover is in a molten blob on the floor. Nothing remains but ashes of my lunch, coat and gloves. About the only thing on old Brownie worth saving are the tires. The fir tree is not significantly harmed but 15 years later, the tree's bark will still have black scorch marks on the side nearest the road.

There's nothing to do but wait until Brownie cools off and no longer presents any kind of danger. We leave the old hulk in the middle of the road, the accurately named emergency brake and transmission thankfully keep it stuck on the hillside. Charlie and I ponder for a moment the idea of Brownie rolling back down the hill, ablaze and smoking, and off into the forest. What a disaster that would be.

We stop at Charlie's place to make a phone call to see if I can find a ride home for the dogs and me. Ron, my friend and neighbor in Bozeman is home and agrees to make the 45 minute drive over the hill to pick us up. While we're waiting Charlie offers me a snort of nerve medicine. Old Overshoes Bourbon is his favorite. It's 10:30 in the morning, but we knock a few back and put the bottle away. In the evening, Nancy calls me from wherever she is on this business trip. "Brownie burned up," I tell her. She doesn't call home again, afraid to hear what other bad news I might have in store for her. When she gets home she tells me her business associates were enthralled with the new adventure story and they all wanted her to call home and get more dirt. She declined.

I tell the mechanic who worked on the carburetor about the fire and he offers to buy Brownie from me and have it towed to his garage. The settlement is not particularly fair but more than the insurance company will give me, so I take it. About a month later, I drop by Charlie's. We spend a few moments admiring my new fourteen year old 1980 F-100 4WD pickup, and I present him with a quart of Jim Beam. He invites me in for a drink, but it's before 10:30 so I politely refuse. It's time to get back to work.

Doug

3

YOU CAN DRIVE A SPIKE WITH A ROCK

All you need in this life is ignorance and confidence;

then success is sure.

--Mark Twain

I can't say with any certainty when it was that we decided we

wanted to build a log cabin. We'd spent the bulk of our lives in Colorado and Montana, and I know that every time we came across a beautiful meadow on a drive along a country road, saw a small clearing around the bend in a hiking trail, or spotted a stand of cottonwoods in a meandering river, we would think, "What a gorgeous spot for a little log cabin."

Long before we decided to build our cabin, our lives revolved around outdoor adventures. We were hikers, first and foremost. We backpacked in the pristine national forests of Montana, Colorado and Washington and the rusty slickrock canyons of Utah. When I met Nancy, I gave up alpine skiing and we began cross-country skiing together, partially because it was so much cheaper to pursue given the price of lift tickets and alpine equipment. We were enthusiastic rafters and took trips on the Green, the Colorado, the Yellowstone, the Tongue (in canoes), the Middle Fork of the Flathead, the Wenatchee and the Stillwater among a few others. We bicycled to work and for recreation. We took long and short tours. We made a shakedown trip with new bicycles and panniers around the San Juan Islands in Washington State, in preparation for a three-month long bicycle tour of England, Wales, Ireland, Scotland, France, Belgium and the Netherlands.

In the 1980s, we discovered the old ranger cabins in the national forests of Montana. In the Gallatin National Forest in particular, we found we could rent, for $25 a night, old patrol cabins in absolutely stunning locations. Each winter we'd go to the Forest Service office in Bozeman and reserve one of the cabins. Some of them you could drive to, others were a long day's ski trek with loaded packs. Others were somewhere in between. The cabins were simple affairs; a collection of sleeping cots, some candles or lanterns, a woodstove for heat, generally a cookstove and a wash basin or some kind of sink, and mismatched pots and dinnerware. Some of them were one room, some with a loft, some with a bedroom. The Forest Service always supplied the cabins with firewood and a cold, clear mountain creek burbled a short walk from the front door. No indoor plumbing meant hauling water from the creek and making short trips to the nearby outhouse, but it was a small price to pay.

These cabins are what made winter-time trips possible for us. We found cooking dinner on a cookstove with a crackling fire, and a night in a sleeping bag on a lumpy old mattress in a modest cabin to be heads and tails above cooking on a portable stove in a cramped and cold tent.

Our careers revolved around the outdoors as well. Nancy and I worked for years in the outdoor equipment industry for firms such as Frostline Kits, Early Winters, Roffe Sportswear, Gerry Outdoor Sports, Kletterwerks, Dana Design and a couple of others, most of which are long gone. My role was as a graphic designer or art director and Nancy worked either as a purchasing agent or industrial seamstress.

Later on, we would find ourselves working as Park Service Rangers in Yellowstone National Park, the first park, "the mother park". We started out in the fee collection operation at the South Entrance, and graduated to Interpretation and Resource Management. As rangers, Nancy and I were lucky enough to visit some of the most spectacular places in Yellowstone, mostly unknown to the average visitor, including the Patrol Cabins at Fox Park, Harebell, Peale Island, Heart Lake, Union Falls and Shoshone Lake. These cabins are not open to the public. The only way to spend a night there is by being a Park Service employee or volunteer, or perhaps a US Senator.

Nancy and I got lucky in the early fall of 1995 and accompanied a couple of old-time rangers on a five day horse-pack trip. I rode a horse named Jackpot. Nancy was on Harvey. The purpose, other than just to have rangers in the backcountry during hunting season, was to build a porch floor using lumber left over from bridge and trail building. We heard amazing old ranger stories all day while riding or working; and lying in bed at night we heard stories about angry grizzly bears.

I'm pretty sure it was the National Park Service (NPS) patrol cabins that truly fired our imaginations and confirmed our belief we could build one ourselves. These cabins, like their Forest Service counterparts, were built by non-professional builders. In a lot of cases, they were constructed by Civilian Conservation Corps (CCC) crews in the 1930s. I'm positive there was no architect masterminding these cabins; maybe someone drew a sketch, maybe not. I can rather easily visualize a series of mule trains hauling in construction materials; a load of concrete for the nominal foundation, bundles of shingles and a cask of nails for the roof, a woodstove broken down into a jumble of cast iron plates with a burlap sack containing some nuts and bolts. I know most cabins were built with two man cross-cut saws and axes, rather than chain saws. Rough calloused hands surely peeled logs with an old-fashioned drawknife, swung an ax to cut a rough notch, cranked a brace and bit to drill a hole in a log or door, and hammered nails into cedar shingles on the roof. Well, I knew if those old timers could build a cabin using hand tools only, I could build one with those same tools, along with a chain saw and a pickup truck.

I've been asked many times since, "Where did you get enough confidence to take on that project?" Starting in 1967, after graduation from high school I worked three summers at Winter Park Ski Area in Colorado. I was a member of one of two trail crews that cleared new ski slopes. Over time, I learned practically everything there is to know about chainsaws. I can confess that I never got very good at sharpening a chainsaw chain by hand because there was a dedicated individual that did that for us and we'd each bring him two or three dull chains every afternoon. But we did a passable job in an emergency, sitting in the grass or on a stump, filing away, putting a new sharper edge on each tooth. Dropping a tree in a pre-selected spot and bucking it up into a burn pile was totally unremarkable, it was what we did Monday through Friday. I learned to use "wedges and sledges" to direct a tree's fall if it happened to lean the wrong way. But mostly we had the luxury of dropping the tree wherever it wanted to go.

Each evening when we got to the shop at the base of the slopes, we took our saws apart and cleaned them with an air hose or brush and solvent and put them back together. Or you cleaned out the truck, or prepared the gas mixture for the next day, or just shot the shit with other guys. We worked in teams of two, one sawing and one stacking the bucked up tree for an hour and then we'd switch. I learned how to not get your sawbar pinched and stuck while cutting and limbing a dropped tree. If your sawbar became stuck, and you couldn't extricate it with muscle alone, another team would have to stop what they were doing to come over, make a few cuts with their saw to release yours. I struggled to keep the chain sharp, mostly by keeping it out of the rocks, dirt and duff on the hillside.

During those three summers I earned a buck and a quarter an hour, normally wore one pair of Levi's for five days straight, along with a clean t-shirt and blue work shirt every day. The hard hats they gave us never made it out of the truck onto our heads. My boots were toast by the end of the summer. The first day of work, I took only one sandwich and hunger gnawed at me all afternoon. The second day, I took two and it still wasn't enough. Eventually, I found out that four sandwiches were too many; they made me drowsy and sluggish for the first part of the afternoon. During those summers I learned a lot and not just about chainsaws. But when you consider that a chainsaw is the most basic tool of a present day cabin builder, it was very valuable experience and time well spent.

In ensuing summers I worked on a construction crew in Denver putting up an apartment building. My father told me to tell them I was a journeyman framer, and with some misgivings, I did. They hired me but no doubt thought it suspicious that I would show up on the first day without tools or a tool belt. After my first half an hour of framing with borrowed hammer, tape measure, square and pencil, I got busted. I spent the remainder of the summer as a common laborer sweeping floors, hauling plywood, shoveling dirt, and unloading shingles from railcars. I learned, however, the way in which a building was framed, sheathed, plumbed, wired and drywalled and a little about finish carpentry. I didn't know exactly how to do it, but now I knew the sequence of events.

I learned enough to be hired on by a college friend of mine in Crested Butte as the third man in his construction company of three people. I was the low man on the totem pole but it was fascinating work. We built houses from scatch, doing every task with the exception of the plumbing and electricity. Bill had a small bulldozer that was our earthmover and forklift so I learned to drive a tracked vehicle. I watched Bill scoop out a crawlspace and we began setting forms for the footer and foundation walls. I discovered that geometry and the Pythagorean Theorum have very practical applications. I learned how to work concrete and lay block. I made trips to Gunnison in the 4WD Chevy flatbed to purchase lumber and learned how to reject boards with a warp, a wane or loose knots. I knew how to strap it down to survive the trip back to the worksite. I became proficient in the use of a Skilsaw, learned how to frame a wall, how to shingle a roof with cedar shingles, how to hang sheetrock, how trim a door or window. Granted, I couldn't do all of these things very well, but I now understood the basics of building a house. I didn't know it then, but I was learning to build a cabin.

Later on, in 1980, Nancy and I would get married and buy a house, and with our limited income, it seemed only natural that we would attempt to fix it up ourselves. We were too poor to feel good about buying tools, so our toolbox consisted of a hammer, a few screwdrivers, a chisel or two, and a knock-off K-Mart 'skilsaw', and not much else. Our first house in Manhattan, Montana was a fixer-upper built in the late 1880s. Among other things, it lacked any insulation whatsoever. Winters are long, cold and dark in Montana, so we bought a woodstove. In the showroom I saw a beautiful stove hearth constructed of used red brick, and I just knew I could build one like it. So I did. My hearth lacked a certain sophistication; each course of red brick tended to diminish slightly in width so it had a noticeable taper at the top. I didn't have a level and didn't think of using a homemade plumb bob, but all in all, it was successful. The hearth kept the woodstove from setting the wall ablaze, and the bricks soaked up heat and radiated it back into the house long after the fire went out. And it was rather handsome. Fifteen years later I would build one just like it, only better. With a level.

The staircase was another matter. Our one-bedroom house in Manhattan had a strange feature. The flight of stairs coming down from the second story, where there was something resembling a second bedroom, ended at a landing. Unfortunately, from the landing you had to exit through one of two doors; one led into the only bathroom and the other went into the bedroom. Why someone would actually design and construct something like this, we never figured out. As you can imagine, this laughable access to the second bedroom made having houseguests a problem.

Our solution was to rip out the stairway and install a new one that came down into the living room. I drew up a plan, ran it by Nancy, worked up my courage and drove to the lumberyard and placed my order. The lad that helped me overload my pickup asked in all innocence, "Whatcha buildin'? A bridge?" I ended up building a bridge, I mean a staircase, that would not have looked out of place in a massive ski lodge or an old barn. The stringers were 3x12 rough sawn fir and the treads were a full dimension 2x10, planed but not sanded. I suppose the stairway might have looked perfectly at home in a log cabin somewhere. But it was sturdy; I probably could have taken an obliging horse up that set of stairs.

To feed that woodstove I mentioned, we went out into the Gallatin National Forest and cut our own firewood. From a neighbor who worked as a logger, I bought a used chainsaw. Gary had used it hard for two or three years and it was now worn out and expendable. It was a Jonsereds, and the bar was 24 inches long - way too long for cutting firewood, but perfect for felling big Montana Douglas Firs. The Jonsereds was heavy and balky, would tire you out long before you could collect a cord of wood, and wouldn't start reliably, but I loved it and used it for many seasons.

Over the years, one of the most valuable lessons I have learned is that you can't have too many tools and you can't read enough books on the task at hand. Ask any one who has ever built anything, no matter how insignificant, they know that proper tools make the task at hand easier and more successful. You can drive a spike with a rock or a tack hammer, but it's easier and faster with a three pound sledge. Tools are not a substitue for skill, knowledge or patience but a counterpart to them. I wasn't ready to build a cabin just yet. I had the basic skill set and could learn the rest, but I still lacked most of the tools and the land. And books. Books on how to build a log cabin.

Doug

4

CHOMPIN' AT THE BIT

Buy land. They're not making it anymore.

--Mark Twain

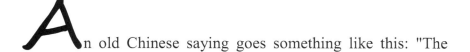n old Chinese saying goes something like this: "The

journey of ten thousand miles begins with the first step." It is credited to Lao Tzu, the founder of Taoism. Our own journey, the dream of building and owning a log cabin, has a very obvious beginning point. The beginning is that we need somewhere to build it, some land to build upon.

Early in 1993, we scour southwestern Montana searching for property. On weekends we drive around looking at vacant land and any cabins we think we might find interesting. Almost every piece of real estate falls into one of three categories. One, the previous owner had already screwed up everything to the point where we don't want to undertake the mess it has become. Or two, it is too expensive. And three, there are properties, generally raw land, that are fairly pristine, but have no view or are devoid of trees.

Finally, one day in April we see an ad in a real estate magazine, touting parcels of land northwest of Livingston in the Bangtail Mountains. Lost Springs it is called, and prices are right. It is actually a subdivision made up of old grazing and forest land sandwiched between the national forest and a deeded ranch.

We call the agent and he informs us we can't see it until June. Right now it is inaccessible due to snow. We tell him we will try to ski or snowshoe in and look over the property, so he gives us some directions, faxes us a map of the parcels of land and a price list. We drive as far as we can in the car and get out. A snowmobile track goes off up the road and disappears around the corner. It seems that we have about a mile and a half walk, so off we go.

The snow is in patches here and there, and where it remains it is hard and crusty due to freezing and thawing so it's an easy but slippery walk. We spend the day wandering around the subdivision orienting ourselves to the map, using the rudimentary road as our guide. We feel pretty sure we have found where we want to be, we just have to find the parcel we like the best. Finally, we realize parcel 26 is the one that best suits our needs. The road curves around the southeast part of the 21 acre lot, and without walking the property lines, we can guess that it's full of trees. It has a pretty spectacular view, not as good as another parcel over the ridge to the south, but the wind isn't blowing right here. Over at the other parcel, it was howling ferociously. At this parcel it's sheltered just enough so the famous Livingston and Yellowstone Valley wind is going right over the top of us. There are small open areas with the grass sticking out of the snow, heavily forested north facing slopes, and a small rocky cliff face for a little drama. Near the little cliff there is a spot that seems like it will make a great cabin site. South facing slopes are already free of snow, and we can look at the north end of the Absarokas. For the modest price, we feel we've found the perfect piece of land.

We understand the detracting elements of the property and actually appreciate them rather than find them drawbacks. The rudimentary road means less traffic and less chance of unmitigated development. No power lines will make most people think twice, or three times before they buy up here. No phone lines means privacy and again, a slower rate of development. In short, it's not exactly a wilderness, but it feels like it.

We look at each other and nod. This is the place. We hustle on down the hill into town. For some inexplicable reason we're worried that this parcel will be snatched away from us. Other than the snowmobile tracks we saw earlier, no one has been up here for months, with the exception of some coyotes and elk. But we imagine a line of buyers waiting at the desk of the real estate agent, all of them waving wads of cash, trying to outbid each other for our piece of property.

Back in Livingston, we go see the real estate agent, but the office is closed for the day. Still paranoid about somehow losing out on this property, we leave a note of our intentions, and head back over the hill to Bozeman.

Monday morning, we talk to Chuck in the sales office and it turns out they won't let us complete the sale until we can walk the property boundaries with the sales agent. Since it's April and there's still a fair amount of snow, we're going to have to wait a month or more. Furthermore, Chuck won't go up there until we can drive his Dodge Ram to the first corner stake. We're chompin' at the bit, but there is nothing we can do but wait.

The first week in June, Chuck calls us and we make an appointment to meet him and walk the property boundaries. Our guesses about the parcel are quite correct. First, there is not a decent sized level space anywhere. Second, Lost Springs is not a misnomer, at least on our parcel, or they are very well hidden. We're buying 21 acres of Douglas Fir and the view from the top corner stake of the property is absolutely stunning. All things considered, we're in love with the parcel. We have worked out the details of the loan, so we sign on the dotted line. Suddenly, we feel like land barons.

Nancy

5

UNDER THE SPELL OF THE

ROCKY MOUNTAINS

I hate to think that all my current experiences
will someday become stories with no point.
--Bill Watterson, <u>Calvin and Hobbes</u>

Doug was born in Colorado. I wasn't. I couldn't wait to

move away from the Midwest. Sometimes I think there is an error
on my birth certificate. A geographical conundrum, it pretends I was

born in Chicago, of all places. My actual growing up, however, slid over the state line into Indiana, an area called the Calumet Region: the land of oil refineries and steel mills. I ventured west at age 20. I felt 'The Region' pushing me away. I was a fish out of water.

Each summer, from the time I was a wee sprout, my parents, my brother and usually a rotating cousin piled into the family sedan, a '55 Ford Fairlane. The car top carrier and trunk were packed so expertly by my mother, that we rarely had to resupply over the two or three weeks we traveled.

Family camping equipment in the 1950s – 1960s came from one place---Sears, Roebuck & Co. My parents pored over the catalog, working out the details of the equipment order---tent, poles, tarp, sleeping bags and air mattresses, Coleman camp stove, lantern, and more. For our family, shopping at Sears Roebuck also included clothing, all clothing. My mother chose my camping wardrobe, consisting of pedal pushers, several plaid shirts, Keds, and some sort of a hat that matched my father's chic pork pie headgear. Now I was ready to conquer the Badlands, Black Hills, Algonquin Provincial Park, Acadia or Rocky Mountain National Parks.

I'm sure the real motivation behind the camping instead of moteling, was a desire to save money rather than love of camping. But my parents wanted us to see the country, and camping in national forests and national parks was the most frugal way to accomplish it. We would load into the car long before dawn, and my father would put the pedal to the metal for 800 miles before stopping for the evening. He must have been a long-haul trucker in a former life.

When we finally stiff-legged it out of the vehicle at our campsite, we all had chores. The tent had to be pitched properly against wind and rain. Water had to be hauled for dinner and breakfast. My mother expertly handled setting up the camp kitchen. Then, and only then, were we released. As a city kid, these camping trips were a springboard into adventure and freedom not part of my usual routine. Everything was a first for me. Like climbing. In the Badlands one evening before dinner, I attempted to pull myself up to a little bluff, and managed to plant my full palm smack down on a cactus. I howled and immediately brushed off the cactus spikes flat with the skin, the worst treatment possible. But, for months after that incident, I could point to those festerings as a badge of honor.

My first two years of college are a blur, mainly because I attended very few classes. I do know that I transformed, within a week, from a preppy high schooler into a hippie college student with all the suspect attributes. I was on scholarship and work study, and always sensed that coming from the Calumet Region to the Ivy League school of the Midwest was a stigma. By 1970 I was more than a little disillusioned. I dropped out. I worked at a huge law firm in the Chicago Loop for a trial attorney and lived with a couple friends from school. One day, I was called in to the Personnel Office. Mini skirts and hot pants were all the rage at the time. I was wearing knee-length culottes which were unexplainably on the "do not wear" list. They sent me home and told me not to return until I had changed into something more acceptable. I put on a pin-stripe suit, red tie, white button-down shirt, and returned to the Personnel Office and proffered my resignation. This fish was finished swimming upstream.

A college friend, Eileen, had immigrated to Colorado, after a hitchhiking trip across the country. She resumed her schooling 'out west' and didn't take long to experience that 'Rocky Mountain High'. I joined her in the middle of winter. The skies were crystalline blue, and some days we could sit outside in the sun. People actually smiled and said, "Hello". Hello to a perfect stranger? Pieces started falling into place. I bought my first car, a '63 Chevy Bel Air station wagon, found a couple passengers on a ride board in Boulder, and hit the road for The Region. I would return to Colorado in a few weeks, after tying up loose ends, to start paying rent and get a job.

When a description of your possessions includes the four albums to your name, it's easy to understand how simple it was to move. I took the first job I could find, and made sure it was 180 degrees from my former work as a legal secretary. I succeeded. I labored as an agricultural worker at a rose greenhouse. Agricultural wage was less than minimum wage. I made $1.35 per hour, and sometimes worked 10 or more hours per day, depending upon the fickle nature of the roses.

Life in Colorado just seemed to lure one to adventure. Eileen and I didn't want to keep living in the university apartment during the summer session, and were searching for options. We had recently discovered two books that became our direct route into adventure, or at least experimental adventure. One was Alicia Bay Laurel's <u>Living on the Earth</u>, a compendium of one-page hand-illustrated instructions for making and constructing absolutely anything of real importance. For instance, we experimented with dandelion wine, bean sprouts, tire tread sandals, and yogurt. Every one of these failed for one reason or another. The dandelion wine rotted in the plastic garbage can in the bedroom, we quickly forgot the bean sprouts under the bed, and we didn't realize most tires had steel-belted treads that couldn't be cut with tin snips, much less a kitchen knife.

The other book became our bible; Reginald and Gladys Laubin's <u>The Indian Tipi</u>. There was probably a time that I could recite this book backward and forward. I dreamed about it's illustrations. I couldn't study it enough. Eileen and I started plotting our summer. If we had a tipi, and a place to pitch it, we could live in it. The rest would happen on its own. Simple plan, simple execution. So we thought. The only canvas we could locate was mustard yellow and impregnated with wax, definitely not the stuff of the classic Sioux tipi. But it was available and the price was right.

Since there was no way I was going to sew this by hand, I rented a Singer portable sewing machine from the local shop for $5.00 a week. With lots of help, we marked and cut the pieces out in a nearby parking lot. The little sewing machine clogged up with wax, broke needles, and regularly went on strike attempting to sew through many layers of blue jean thick canvas. I hauled it back to the shop and asked them to fix it, week after week. Never once did they ask what in blue blazes was I sewing. As I sewed strip to strip on the 18 foot diameter Sioux tipi, the volume of material took up most of the tiny apartment living room. I moved the sewing machine over to the window and hoisted the bulk of the fabric outside on the lawn. I had nothing to compare my progress to except the illustrations in the book, so I kept soldiering on. Upon completion, it weighed nearly 70 pounds.

We needed land on which to pitch the tipi, and soon. We asked everyone we knew. Word of mouth eventually came through, and a Colorado State University professor who had some property up in the foothills gave us a go-ahead and directions, which included a walk of about a mile. We had no idea where to find tipi poles, which needed to be only about 4 inch butt diameter, up to 28 feet long, and tapered. We were getting down to the wire, and we opted for a very unsightly alternative. We purchased corral poles, already peeled, but horrendously chunky in appearance. Oh well, I didn't think any real Sioux would ever see this tipi.

The day finally came to erect the tipi. It went up quite gracefully, according to plan, just as the Laubins promised. Except for the atrocious color and thick poles, it was marvelous and I was as proud as a mother could be. It was ours. Home sweet home.

I continued working at what I called the "rose factory" that summer, earning my less than minimum wage. Eileen's younger 16-year old sister was shipped out to Colorado to join us, her parents oblivious to what eye-opening experiences their young daughter would behold. She became our daily gopher, having just received her driver's license. MJ dropped me off at work, Eileen at school, and then proceeded to run errands until it was time to reverse the pick up order.

Well before the days of Sun Showers, we encountered the logistics of showering on a regular basis. There was a rickety and rusty old shower at the rose factory, and I obtained permission to shower either before or after work, and keep a stash of toiletries there. Eileen and MJ went to the gym at the university. Nevertheless, our clothes always wafted an aroma of campfire smoke about us, which no amount of laundering could remove.

That summer at the tipi we subsisted primarily on one-pot meals, pancakes, and sandwiches---a culinary wasteland. We had help constructing a raised kitchen area between three trees, a latrine, a huge fire pit, and a tripod for the 55 gallon canvas water bag. Our furniture included some broken down, legless webbed lawn chairs that we found discarded by the side of the road. There was no running water and every gallon we used was another gallon we had to carry up on our backs. It was mandatory for anyone coming up for a visit to bring water. A couple friends drove up one night in their Jeep and brought two 5 gallon Jerry cans of water. That would top off the water bag. Little did we know until way too late that the Jerry cans had a prior history of transporting gasoline. We were too stingy to drain the bag, but we often felt that if we struck a match near our mouths, we might ignite.

We hated to see summer's end, knowing it signaled a move back to town. But the experiment, if one could call it that, had certainly made me a convert. All the nights sitting around the campfire, the moonlight hikes, the coyotes yipping endlessly, the discovery of animal scats---this would not have been possible if I hadn't left the Midwest and if I hadn't sewn this tipi. That I knew for sure. I was under the spell of the Rocky Mountains.

Over the next 20 years, between repeated forays returning to college and graduate school, I found a niche working for outdoor recreational equipment and clothing manufacturing companies. It was at one of these companies in the late 1970s that I met Doug. Together we rafted the Colorado, backpacked the Flat Tops, cross-country skied Jones Pass, and hiked Canyonlands. Every weekend, we loaded Doug's old red Dodge pickup, Midnight, with backpacks, bicycles, raft and oars, and off we went. When the family-owned company we worked for sold out to a corporate giant, we saw the proverbial handwriting on the wall and headed north to Montana.

Nearly 20 years later and about 1,000 credits after beginning my college education, I envisioned myself on a career path. In 1989, I landed a great job at Montana State University in Bozeman as a Project Director in the Extension Service. I quickly became a workaholic; I wrote grant proposals, attended conferences, presented papers, and conducted outreach training sessions. All went swimmingly for six years.

A perk of university employment is reduced tuition, and as long as it didn't conflict with my job I was encouraged to pursue a Master's program. An internship at the Museum of the Rockies opened up in the summer of 1993. The museum's claim to fame are dinosaurs, Plains Indians, and wolves. I met with the Director of Education and proposed sewing and constructing an 18 foot Sioux tipi on the museum grounds. We discussed erecting it on site and allowing museum patrons to enjoy the tipi for three weeks. After that time, it became my property. I made a 3 foot scale model as a hook for my meeting. With very few questions, the project received a thumbs-up.

Every Friday, I wheeled my scale model, display boards and industrial sewing machine outside the museum entrance. This time around, assembly was much easier. I had a more powerful sewing machine, the proper canvas and I was familiar with the construction. I sat under an eave of the building; but being Montana, there were days I battled blowing rain and wind. A few times a campfire would have been the ticket. I interacted with museum patrons, talked about my project and answered questions. On the day of the tipi raising, a Blackfoot elder participated in the ceremony. At the end of the three weeks, Doug and I unceremoniously took the tipi up to our recently-purchased property, where now, we would have a roof over our heads for the occasional overnight.

My job at the University, a USDA-funded program, requires a partnership with a non-profit agency. No non-profit partner, no funding. I come to dread the annual budget brawl, where we grovel for the pittances that are doled out. On a gorgeous February morning in 1995, as I ride my bike to campus, my stomach is already churning. The meeting doesn't go well right from the start. I hold myself responsible. Without warning, I suddenly announce that I am resigning at the end of March. Then I excuse myself, walk out of the building and breathe deeply for the first time in a long spell.

When I get up the nerve to tell my father that I quit my benefit-laden university job for possible seasonal employment, am going to live in a tipi (again) and build a log cabin, his response is, "I should have never taken you on that first camping trip." Well, Dad, I'm glad that you did. But it breaks my heart that you were never able to see the cabin.

Doug

6

STINK MAKES THEM BAD

Sometimes I sits and thinks, and sometimes I just sits.

--Satchel Paige

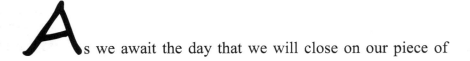s we await the day that we will close on our piece of

property, we struggle to contain our enthusiasm. I want to begin building right away, cutting trees, pounding stakes, digging holes, anything to show some progress. Of course it's not a good idea to go off and begin altering a piece of land that you don't own, but if the road was clear and dry, instead of clogged with snow and mud, I would have been up there doing something. Nancy and I have agreed to spend some time camping on the land, anyway, seeing where the sun rises and sets. Getting a feel for the place before we pick a cabin spot.

So I decide to begin at the beginning and build the most essential and important structure that will sit on that property, ever. I commit myself to building an outhouse in the backyard, one I can then take apart and haul up there in Old Blue, our old beater pickup. Nothing shouts "civilization" better than an outhouse. We will be sleeping on the ground in our tipi, cooking dinner on a campfire but I'm damned if I'm going to squat over a hole to shit. I get out the yellow legal pad and a pencil and begin drawing, thinking about all the outhouses I've ever known and what made them good. And more importantly what made them bad.

Stink made them bad. Spiders made them unpleasant. Lack of a toilet seat made it unsanitary, and for a big guy like me, the height must be comfortable. A toilet paper holder is a must. A magazine rack is essential. And finally, cleanliness is next to Godliness, and just as important in an outhouse.

We make a visit to the Park County Building Department, and learn that there are no building permits required outside of incorporated cities. We're bound only by the covenants attached to the subdivision which don't restrict us from having a temporary outhouse.

First, I scrounge through our old barn. We live near downtown Bozeman, but the place was built before cars and has a ramshackle barn that I use as a workshop. We've lived in the house six years and I still find useful old things in the barn all the time. I turn up an antiquated toilet paper holder, some discarded 3 inch aluminium vent pipe, a couple bundles of asphalt shingles and a six panel door with about four coats of peeling paint on it.

I draw up a plan, head for the lumberyard in Old Blue and bring home a sheet of 3/4 inch plywood and a dozen 2x4s, two sheets of T-111 siding, some 16d nails, and pardon the expression, a 3 inch "Chinaman's" cap.

When Saturday morning arrives, I take my hot steaming coffee out to the backyard near the door of the barn and begin building my outhouse. Nancy has gone to the garage sales with the instructions to not return without a toilet seat. I begin sawing and hammering, all the while paying attention to the fact that it must be portable. I'm using long drywall screws in critical places so that it will come apart and go back together with the Makita battery powered drill.

I raise the four walls and begin working on the first peaked roof I've ever constructed. No shed-roofed outhouse for me. I go easy on myself and go for a 9/12 pitch. I'll never have to get up on it, so why not? I cut one little rafter from a 2x4, copy it and cut another. I screw them together and try them out. They fit, so I make several more. As it turns out, this is very good practice for later on. This little outhouse will have foot-wide eaves all the way around to protect it from the elements. I use Simpson rafter ties and screws to make it easy and portable. In a few weeks, once I get the outhouse put together in its final resting place, I will add a few nails.

By Sunday afternoon, I have a beautiful outhouse in the backyard. It's painted bright green and has a six panel door. A little flue protrudes from the roof. It extends down into the waste chamber and is designed to provide a way for foul odors to escape. The little "Chinaman's" rain cap sits on top of the pipe. There are no shingles, only 30# felt, but it won't take long to roof when it arrives at our property. It has eye-hook latches on the inside and outside of the door so it doesn't flap in the wind. Up in the gable is a screened vent for more ventilation. The ancient toilet paper holder is screwed to the wall. A "Victoria's Secret" catalog rests in the magazine holder. The toilet seat is attached and has a lid. Our outhouse is ready to go for a ride when the time comes.

Monday afternoon, I come home to find neighbors looking across the fence at the outhouse wondering just what the hell is going on. Have we lost our minds? Has our indoor plumbing gone bad?

A few weeks later, we deconstruct the outhouse and load it into the bed of "Old Blue", a '69 Chevy shortbed pickup, 2WD. Someone had started to work on this truck and it has been stripped of chrome and painted a baby blue. When I bought it, I replaced the tiny, welded chain steering wheel with the only decent sized one I could find, which happened to be (egad) bright orange.

When we reach the point where the county road ends and the steep and rutted subdivision road begins, Old Blue begins to struggle. This is the first time we've driven our own vehicle to the property. In the past we've walked the last mile and a half, or rode in the real estate guy's Dodge Ram. Blue has a good old four speed and the load in the short bed helps with traction, but it's a dicey proposition getting Blue to parcel 26. We come down the stretch we will one day call Flame Out Bend, crawling down in compound low and I wonder if we'll be able to get Old Blue back out again. In any case, we make it to our destination. Nancy and I jump out and leave Blue in the middle of the road with the keys in it in case someone needs to get around us, but no one drives by the entire day.

Together, we haul the four walls up the hill, one by one. We grab the shovel and a pick and begin looking for the perfect spot, one shaded by a stand of fir, to reconstruct our little green outhouse. It takes all day to pick the spot, dig the deepest hole we can given the bedrock we run into, put our outhouse back together, level it up with rocks, and shingle the roof. We install the toilet paper we brought onto the toilet paper holder, Nancy goes in and sits down and becomes the first to use our brand new, old fashioned outhouse.

Time would confirm the fact: it is a wonderful structure. It never really smells bad. The vent works perfectly exhausting the odors, along with regular applications of wood ash. It never leaks, the toilet paper never gets wet and flies never seem to infest the interior. In short it's perfect.

We congratulate ourselves, head back to Old Blue and head for home. A half a mile from our property is the aforementioned Flame Out Bend, a steep rocky hill with two hairpin curves. The Montana gumbo has some loaf-of-bread sized rocks and ruts deeper than the axle. Most days it's no problem at all for a 4WD to crawl up the hill in 2nd gear, low range without spinning a tire. But it takes three tries for Old Blue, unloaded, to get up the hill. Finally speed is our ally and we reach the top, tires spinning and mud flying. If we need to try a fourth time, we'll need to fill the bed with 500 pounds of rocks and crawl up in compound low. Tire chains will work but we don't have any with us. It's as plain as day, Old Blue's days are numbered. This truck will need to be replaced with a 4WD pretty soon.

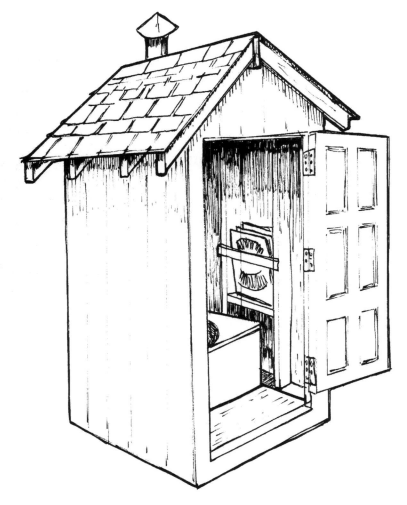

The Outhouse

In a few weeks, I'm back again, still in Old Blue. The road has dried out a little and I've got a new set of tire chains so I don't worry about getting home. Today, I've come alone and brought a pile of lumber. Some of it new, some used and some of it salvaged from various places. In the back of the pickup is a little window I found in an alley, and a bunch of used tongue and groove siding that was given to me. I've got hammer and nails, a hand saw and a few other carpentry tools. I've already cut a bunch of scrap plywood at home. I'm going to build a shed for storing tools, sleeping bags, foam pads, kerosene, everything we don't want to haul around, back and forth.

Once again, I park Blue in the middle of the road and haul all the materials up to the selected spot, between the tipi site and the outhouse. I spend the next three, four days building a shed. Because there is not one single flat spot larger than a sheet of plywood on the property, it has to be built on 4x4 piers. When I'm done I have a 6 foot x 8 foot shed with a little window. It has a lovely pitched roof, nails to hang tools from and a padlock on the door. Over time this simple shed will become our camp kitchen for a couple of seasons, get re-roofed and re-sided and put on skids and moved down the hill closer to the cabin site and go back to its original purpose as a storage shed.

But, before we can begin working on our cabin, we need a few more tools, a reliable 4WD truck and more importantly, we need to pick a spot on which to build.

Doug

7

IT ONLY HAS TO LAST A COUPLE HUNDRED YEARS

Mistakes are part of being human. Appreciate your mistakes for what they are: precious life lessons that can only be learned the hard way. Unless it's a fatal mistake, which, at least, others can learn from.

--Al Franken, "Oh the Things I Know," 2002

*I*n the late summer of 1994, I, along with my neighbor Ron, an

architecture professor at Montana State University, go up to the property and pour the first corner pad. It sounds like a very simple undertaking, and by all rights, it should be. But before it's possible to pour the first footer, I need to know where to put it. That means I need to have a cabin design. And we have to get its footprint transferred onto the ground.

As I've said before, our imagination has produced a cabin similar to the Forest Service and Park Service cabins we are acquainted with. We've planned to collect water off the roof, and light will be from candles and kerosene lamps. Early on, we'd gotten a price from our electric co-operative and decided bringing in electricity was not in the cards. We've talked to neighbors in Lost Springs and found out wells in that neck of the woods are very deep and therefore very expensive. We are not even sure a well drilling rig can get to the property. In short, we are prepared to live off-the-grid, with no washer and dryer, no running water, no baseboard heat. However, it has never been our intention to have anything more than a weekend cabin where we can sit on the porch and watch the sunset rather than *Seinfeld*.

Earlier, I happened to be taking a class in Auto-CAD, the computer aided technical drawing program. As my final project I produced a floor plan, and an east, west, north and south elevation.

The strength of a CAD produced drawing program is the precise 90 degree corners, the perfectly straight lines, the impeccable circles. Conversely, it doesn't do a very good job of drawing an object that ends up just slightly out of plumb, a little more of a rhombozoid than a perfect rectangle. It doesn't replicate hand peeled Douglas Fir logs that are knotty and gnarly and tapered butt to tip. In other words, the CAD does an unsatisfactory job drawing a real log cabin. I've drawn a more handsome and realistic representation with a pencil on a legal pad. The CAD drawn version looks like something that would come out of a factory, with milled logs absent of knots, the butt and tip ends the same exact diameter. The CAD version looks like a cabin made of Lincoln Logs, no disrespect intended toward the good people at that outfit.

The foundation plan, however, looks fantastic. The dimensions are charted out for me, 32 feet here and 26 feet there, with little perfectly formed arrows. The sill logs are exactly the same width and the corner footers all exactly the same size. The diagonals are calculated for me at 41.2 feet and change. It calculates the distance between footers for me; 16 feet 6 inches here and 15 feet 6 inches there. Incredible indeed. The problem, however, is that I have a cabin site that slopes off to the north and east. The southwest corner is my high point and the northeast corner needs to be around eight feet off the ground if our cabin is to have a level floor.

The cabin building book by Monte Burch, the Complete Guide to Building Log Homes, tells me that log cabins don't necessarily

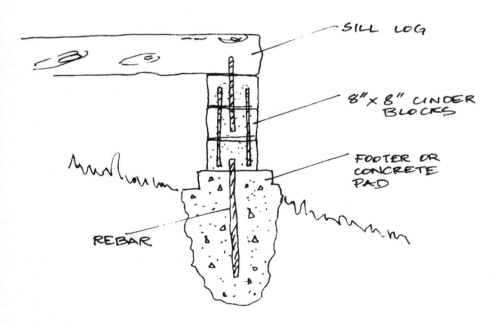

need a concrete or block foundation underneath the entire structure. This is good news. Thousands of two-hundred year old cabins still exist and they sit solidly on a big flat rock at each corner. In fact, most all the weight of a log cabin rests on the corners, and in our case, a couple of mid-points. A perfect rectangle of concrete walls sitting on a footer like we built at Bill's construction company in Crested Butte would be wonderful, without a doubt. (It's absolutely essential in stick built homes.) But for our cabin, it's not to be. We haven't even bothered to have the price of one calculated for us. At this point in our lives, money is in short supply and a perimeter foundation, eight feet high at the northeast corner is out of the realm of possibility.

But piers work fine for a log cabin, so piers it will be. We just need to figure out where to place them. Here we stand, Nancy and I, in the middle of our house site early in June, with a hammer, a bundle of stakes and a 100 foot tape measure. We are conscious of a huge fir tree on one side. Further, we're constrained by the rock cliff that we choose to build right next to, where the front porch will cantilever slightly over the void.

We have a calculator so we take measurements and pound stakes and figure the hypotenuse. Miss Sandy Wright, my junior year high school geometry teacher would be so proud. Monsieur Pythagoras himself would be astonished to see us using his theorem on this sunny, green hillside in Montana. $A^2 + B^2 = C^2$. If we can compute a square root, we're in business.

We set our stakes and measure again, until finally, we have what we think is a 26 x 32 rectangle, with the front door facing south and a little east. The front side of the cabin will be in the sun, with a porch sitting on the top of a little cliff. Half of the front porch will be covered and have an unobstructed view of the north end of the Absaroka Range, the Yellowstone River valley and the twinkling lights of Livingston, Montana. The covered half porch on the north side will look down the hill into the grassy floored forest and have a glimpse of the rutted road. The back door will open on to this sheltered porch from the kitchen.

We only need to take down one tree to clear our cabin site. Our goal was to take none, but this is unavoidable. A little later on this summer with the help of my brother-in-law, Tony, we'll drop the tree and turn it into firewood.

Right now, we begin concentrating on digging and pouring our corner pads. Before I come up here with my neighbor Ron, I dig several holes at the four corners as deep as I can. Close to the cliff at the southwest corner, I can get down only a foot before I hit bedrock. On the northeast side I dig, with a pick, a shovel, a post hole digger and a spud bar, a hole that goes down 36 inches. Deep enough, it's below frost level and I call it quits.

I've hauled up our wheelbarrow, a badly used 55 gallon drum full of rusty water and several bags of Ready-Mix concrete, enough to pour a footer or two. I've made several forms out of 1x6 pine that are 16 inches square, and I've cut a bunch of rebar to random lengths.

As an architect, Ron has specified concrete footers in thousands of structures and knows the code like it's printed on his tie, but he's never actually poured one. I've done this before but not lately. We show each other how. We open a couple bags of Ready-Mix and pour it all in the wheelbarrow, add a little rusty, slightly oily water and begin mixing to the perfect consistency. Ron and I debate the effect of the suspect water on the concrete. He tells me about the Roman architects. He describes two thousand year old engineering feats like the Pont du Gard in southern France, and the recipe for concrete that sets up under water that the Romans utilized to make harbors and breakwaters that still exist. We conclude the footers will last a few hundred years, anyway, and that's enough. We add some rebar into the hole, reinforcement that the Romans didn't have, and then the concrete. When the concrete more-or-less fills the hole in the ground, I place the little 3-1/2x16x16 form on top, level it, punch in some rebar that will stick out of the top of the form, and fill it with concrete. We dump the remaining mix in the bottom of an empty hole, and stand back and look at our work. We're pleased with our efforts.

A number of years later, Ron will bring architect friends and visiting professors, from as far away as Moscow and the U.K. to our cabin. Buildings Ron designed are all over Bozeman and some other towns in the U.S. But he would always take his friends over to the southwest corner and proudly show them the footer he poured.

A month or so later, I've poured all the piers and Nancy and I are trying to get the piers, where the first sill logs will eventually sit, to a common elevation. Or level, so to speak. I am too stingy, or too poor, or too stupid to own a transit, much less rent one for a few days, hence we're relying on necessity who is the mother of invention. I read about this trick in the Monte Burch book. We are using a 1/2 inch clear plastic tube about 40 feet long filled half with water and half with red wine. The wine is to keep the water from freezing, and we also discover it works great as a visual device, plain water being essentially clear.

"Up about six inches," calls Nancy. I move it up six inches as she requests and blow on my frozen fingers.

"Down about three inches," yells Nancy. I move it down about three inches.

"Up about three inches," screams Nancy. I'm impatient, grumbling and cursing. I move it up three inches.

"Well, damn it, now down about two inches," she says.

I go ballistic. "Make up your fucking mind, for Pete's sake, " I scream as I abruptly stand up with the tube in my hand and lose all the progress we've gained.

Two out of three components of our leveling device are almost as elemental as the earth itself. Water is very basic and nearly as common as dirt. Wine is one of mankind's older and better inventions and makes a passable antifreeze for our work today. The plastic tubing is none of those things, but it does an excellent job anyway.

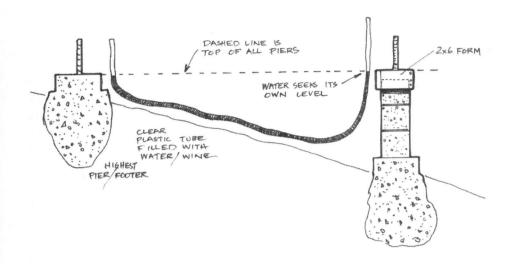

DASHED LINE IS
TOP OF ALL PIERS

2x6 FORM

WATER SEEKS ITS
OWN LEVEL

CLEAR
PLASTIC TUBE
FILLED WITH
WATER / WINE

HIGHEST
PIER / FOOTER

The water/ wine level

The piers are sitting on concrete footers; the footers are at the four corners and in between and are random heights, a few inches above the ground level. The piers themselves are constructed of half cinder blocks, 8 by 8 inches, one atop the other to the most convenient height, and then filled with rebar and concrete. The last few inches will be built up with concrete on top of the cinder blocks. To determine the height of the last few inches of concrete, we are using our primitive but very accurate level. As you probably know, water seeks its own level and wine does too. So as Nancy and I hold our respective ends of the tubes at our respective piers, the water and wine fluctuate for awhile, rising and falling, and eventually settle at the same elevation.

But each time one of us moves their end of the device, the water/wine seeks its own level again, and it may be three inches high or an inch low. When I move my tube up or down, the fluid fluctuates and Nancy has to move her end of the tube to get the water level right at her mark, and on and on. And that's why we're angry with each other. She has her end of the tubing level with the top of the corner pad which is highest in elevation. I'm trying to find the spot on every other footer pad and pier equal to that first one.

Eventually, incrementally, we make progress and we make a mark on each one of the piers and get the little concrete forms that are sitting on top of the blocks, to the proper height. When we pour the concrete and pull off the forms we'll have all the piers at the exact same height above sea level, in theory anyway.

We mix up a batch of concrete, busting the ice off the water bucket as necessary. It's cold on the side of this mountain in late November. My job with the Park Service is over for the season and I won't go back to Yellowstone until May. Between now and then we are trying to get a few things accomplished before winter makes any progress impossible. If the foundation could be done when we return in the spring, it would be a good thing.

We've squandered most of the day, and the light, with other tasks including dinking around getting the tube filled with water and wine (it's harder than it sounds when you forget the funnel). We mix the concrete and pour it into the forms, screeding off the excess and troweling it smooth. Quite quickly a microscopic layer of water forms on top, and the chemical reactions between the lime and the water begin to take place. We move on to the next pier and repeat the action, and do it again until we're forced to mix more cement. The temperature is dropping and the light is going fast.

We finish the eighth and final form with our fingers freezing and the light almost entirely gone. We trudge up the hill and then down to the road where the truck sits, our used, 1980 Ford 4WD half ton pickup, that we call Rusty for no reason other than it is an ugly rust-brown color. We begin the drive back to Bozeman, warming our fingers on the heat blasting from the dashboard.

On the way over the hill, we ask ourselves a bunch of questions. Are we committed to this project? Are we crazy? What are we doing up here with frozen fingers and toes on the side of a mountain?

Traipsing back and forth from Bozeman with only some of our tools, arriving late and leaving early. We haven't really bought all the way into the project yet. Are our efforts sustainable? Will we have enough money to continue? Are some of our friends correct? Are we fools on a fool's errand? Is it stupid for a couple of forty-somethings to consider living in a tipi and building a log cabin from scratch? We ponder these questions.

We are a few months away from totally committing ourselves to this project, we just don't know it yet.

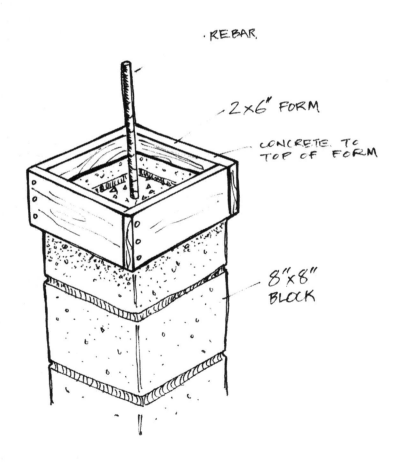

As luck would have it we get some excellent dry and 'warm' weather for a few more weeks. It gives us a chance to begin putting some sill logs in place.

We return to the property one morning and pull off all the forms. We stretch our 100 foot tape measure and discover, to our horror, the diagonals don't match. They should match because it's supposed to be a rectangle. Each half of these two right triangles should together form a rectangle, but they don't. They form a parallelogram if we're lucky, or a rhombozoid maybe, and a four sided polygon if worse comes to worst. We check them again, and once more. When I worked at Bill's construction company, diagonals could be checked before the forms were poured and corrected. A modern dwelling has almost no error in the measurement of the diagonals, and we're off by eight to ten inches. I am totally discouraged. I feel like hanging it up.

We sit down and think about the situation. We're building an old fashioned log cabin the way the Scandinavians did, and the pioneers did. They were working with string marked into cubits or rods or some such, and tools made at a blacksmith's forge accurate to the nearest six inches, give or take. We've read books. We know the pioneers didn't carry around a 100 foot tape measure and a square root calculator. We're sure they didn't draw their plans with a CAD program.

We're probably going to be all right. The materials we're going to be working with are logs, organic as hell, and like snowflakes, no two are alike. Eight to ten inches will be nothing when it's all said and done. In fact, this organic simplicity is part of the charm and the reason we're building it ourselves. If we wanted a house or a log cabin, mass produced in a steel building covering three quarters of an acre, we would have stuck with our original jobs and gotten a mortgage.

We start to feel pretty good about it. We realize we're going to make more mistakes and we'll just have to make the best of it. I know the plywood subfloor will probably take some jimmyin' to make it work, which I can do. And the drywall hanger, me, will be cursing the carpenter, me. And the roofer will probably curse me loudest of all. But it's going to be all right. The logs will be very forgiving.

Doug

8

TWO HORSE HORSEPOWER

It's always been and it always will be the same in the world: The horse does all the work and the coachman is tipped.

-- Anonymous

During the winter of 1995, Nancy and I are engaged in

the process of finding a logger to provide us with the logs to build our cabin. We've even gone so far as to price the purchase and delivery of Lodgepole Pine logs delivered to the site. But it is not to be; we are priced out of the market. Way, way out of the market.

The trees on our property are Douglas Fir, considered an inferior type of house-log compared to Lodgepole. If you've spent some time in the Rockies, you may have noticed different types of conifer forest. Maybe you noticed a forested stand of mixed spruce and fir, similar to a stand on the north shore of Yellowstone Lake between Grant and Lake. I can think of stands of Ponderosa Pine over around Billings, Montana, and impressive stands of Larch or Tamarack along the Montana-Idaho border. Elsewhere in the Southern Rockies there is Cedar, Juniper and Sub-alpine fir. Or perhaps you've seen large stands of Lodgepole Pine all over in Yellowstone and throughout the Rockies. They are considered the premier cabin building log. There are several reasons, but the long, straight, branch-free trunk is the most obvious. I believe someone once described them as a "Christmas tree on top of a telephone pole". The fairly thin bark compared to a Douglas Fir is another reason it is highly prized among cabin builders. Later on, during the log peeling stage, Nancy and I would stare enviously at the tall stands of beautiful thin-barked Lodgepole we saw every day in Yellowstone.

They are called Lodgepole because the plains Indians used to make forays into the foothills of the Rockies to harvest the young saplings for their tipi poles. In fact it's what we used for our tipi. Being long and straight and gently tapered with only a few small branches, they do indeed make perfect lodge poles.

Douglas Fir, however, are studded with branches from tip to butt. Generally, they can be something other than straight and the bark is quite thick compared to a Lodgepole. I don't mean to imply that Doug Fir is a bad tree to build with, just a little harder to deal with. The branches must be trimmed, the thick bark peeled away, and the stub of the branch trimmed again down to the surface of the log. And you can't expect too many perfectly straight logs.

But we have 21 acres of Doug Fir so our cabin will be constructed with them. We just have to find someone who can do the job. In my estimation, it's not so much a job felling the trees as getting them to the cabin site. Because we don't want to trash the building site by getting a conventional logger with motorized equipment, a front end loader or bulldozers and donkey engines, we are searching for a horse logger. Eventually we take the advice of our neighbor, Tom, a horseshoeing instructor at MSU and agree to call a client of his. We phone Elroy, a horse-logger formerly out of Minnesota, and agree to meet him at the end of the county road a few days from now. I am pretty sure Elroy is broke because rather than waiting for spring, he's anxious to go, ASAP.

Elroy is a character, a gentleman of 60 or so. His appearance doesn't inspire confidence at first. He wears a battered cowboy hat over his grey hair, his belly hangs over his belt a little, and he hasn't shaved in a few days. He looks more like a stereotypical truck driver than what I imagined a horse-logger might look like. Alex, his nephew, is a different matter. He's tall, muscular and lean at the same time. He wears a black wool railroader's hat, wool pants, wool plaid shirt and insulated rubber boots. In short, Alex looks like what Hollywood central casting would send over for a North Woods logger. But I quickly learn both Alex and Elroy are the real deal.

It's March and there is very little snow compared to normal, so we are able to walk in and survey the site. I point out two of the corner stakes to Elroy and Alex and provide them with a plat of the land. We stomp around in the snow, while Elroy sizes up the trees and asks questions. Where do I want the logs to end up? What length of logs do I want? What is the ideal girth of the logs? How many did I need? Is there water for the horses somewhere? Do I want him to do anything special with the limbs and tree tops? Do I want the stumps left or cut off at the ground? Do I need him to deal with the horse manure, or could he leave it behind? Do I want to save any particular tree or trees? Is there a particular stand I want saved or an area to be left alone? A lot of questions I hadn't considered.

Elroy gives me a price of $1500 and I agree to it immediately. It seems like a screamin' deal. I tell him I'll write out a check for half as soon as we get back to the truck.

Elroy, for his part says, "We'll start cutting up here in a few days if we don't get any more snow."

Several days later we get a phone call. It's Elroy and true to his word, he asks me if I want to come up to the property the next day, which is by now the middle of March, and see the progress. Nancy and I agree it would be a wonderful sight to see. We tell him we'll make an appearance tomorrow, Saturday. He then asks if I could bring him a check for the final $750.

Elroy, left and Alex, work with Belle and Bobbie. The sill logs are visible in the background and the beginning of the log pile to Elroy's right.

The next morning we arrive at the end of the county road at about 10:00. There is a small log truck with a horse trailer parked at the base of the hill. There are horse tracks in the snow leading up the 4WD road. Each hoof print is the size of a small cake pan, easily twice the measurement of an average horse. We hear the high pitched whine of revved up chainsaws long before we arrive at the cabin site. Elroy and Alex are in the process of limbing a newly fallen tree.

Elroy is wearing a glove on one hand and a dirty, bloody sock on the other. We never get to take a look at it but he tells us he's mangled his fingers somehow. I can imagine about twenty ways to screw up your hand here around the heavy logs, the chainsaws, the horses and harness. There's probably another twenty I don't think of.

Two silver-gray Percheron draft horses, both mares, stand near the outhouse stamping their feet. One is Belle and the other is Bobbie, and I certainly can't tell them apart. One is a youngster and the other a more mature horse, or so Elroy tells me. A decent sized pile of logs sits nearby. They've been working for a couple of days now and have another day or two to go. I ask, and Elroy tells me they ride Bobbie and Belle up and down the hill each morning and night bringing in the gear they need for the day. That is something I would like to see, without a doubt. Still, I can picture Elroy riding a Percheron mare, without a saddle and hauling a gas can with his mangled hand. They stash the chainsaws in the outhouse at night and also keep a running tally of logs on the interior wall. Later we peek in the outhouse and see; four marks and a slash, four marks and a slash, the work is getting done.

The cutting and felling is the easy part. Hauling them to the house site is the more complex part of the job. It turns out Belle is the youngster, she's just learning the trade, and Bobbie is the old hand who has done this a thousand times. Elroy fixes up Bobbie with a riveted leather harness. The harness connects with two straps to a swingletree, a stout bar of wood that then connects to a single chain, then finally the log tongs. Elroy works from ten or so feet behind the horse. In his hands are a long set of leather reins with which he communicates to Bobbie, that and yelling commands. Bobbie hauls about three or four logs to the site one log at a time. It takes them about 15 or 20 minutes per log, depending on how far away they are. Then, Elroy gives the old girl a rest and harnesses up Belle. For a little while, we get to see a minor rodeo, with Elroy at the reins giving commands and Alex at Belle's head trying to reason with her. It's clear Belle is not happy with this arrangement.

Eventually Belle gets one log to the site in 45 minutes to an hour. Elroy then harnesses up Bobbie again. I imagine Elroy spends about the same amount of time with each horse, but Bobbie does three quarters of the work. (No different than any other workplace in America.) Watching this team of four work is one of the most fascinating sights I have ever seen. The process is very basic, it is fundamental and satisfying. Not much has changed for a long, long time. Leather harnesses, steel chains, the sweat of the horses and men, and real, honest to goodness horsepower. Not the internal combustion kind of high torque and speed, but just two-horse horsepower. Only the chainsaws and gas cans give evidence that we are in the last few years of the twentieth century instead of a few hundred years earlier.

At some point during the day, Elroy takes me aside and points to the corner pads, piers and sill logs. He doesn't like the look of my pier foundation and he doesn't mince words.

"That's no way to build a cabin. You better get some experienced help before you go any further," he tells me.

Actually, if it had been financially feasible to construct a standard concrete foundation, I would have done so. There was a popular saying on the Denver condominium building I worked on all those years ago. Whenever some carpenter, plumber or electrician got too fussy, he would hear something like, "Don't worry, man, we ain't building a fucking piano." Well, Nancy and I aren't building the Taj Mahal, merely a cabin that only has to last a couple hundred years or so. In any case, we have no choice, we can only press on.

Nonetheless, I appreciate Elroy's concern and the fine job he and Alex have done. Later on that summer, we are able to look out over the property and see some stumps and branches on the ground. Other than a few clumps of horse manure, and a big pile of logs there is little evidence of a logging crew having worked over the area. I have a hard time imagining what the site would look like if there had been mechanized equipment operating on this north facing slope on a cold March day but I know it wouldn't be pretty. If you're reading this Elroy and Alex, thanks to you and Belle and Bobbie for a fine job. And by the way, the cabin turned out fine.

Bobbie, or is it Belle, and Elroy haul a log up the hill to the pile.

Nancy

9

THERE IS NO WAY TO SUGAR-COAT ABSOLUTE DRUDGERY

As the poet said, 'Only God can make a tree' – probably because it's so hard to figure out how to get the bark on.

--Woody Allen

Yogi Berra said it best, "It's *deja vu* all over again." Here I am, nearly 25 years later, heading off to live in a tipi once more. In the back of the pickup, our backpacks are lined up. Their brands read like my resume: Frostline Kits, Kletterwerks, Dana Design. In the packs are supplies for the coming month: tools, clothing, food for humans and dog, a few pots/pans/utensils, camp stove and lantern, sleeping bags and pads. Hauling these provisions into the cabin site will take all day, who knows how many trips, trudging up and down the hill. We opt to walk rather than ski, since at this time of the year the 4WD road is a mixture of snow drifts, gumbo, and gravel. Therefore we can neither drive, snowmobile or even ski on it.

During my first tipi adventure, my "backpack" was a $5 canvas Boy Scout rucksack from Jax Surplus in Fort Collins, with un-padded cotton web shoulder straps and no frame, interior or exterior. The amount of weight I carried in the pack had a direct correlation to the depth of ridges carved into my shoulders. Our Dana Design backpacks now were cutting edge, designed to handle heavy loads, even tested on Mount Everest. So, except for the fact that I am well into my 40's, I shouldn't be whining. At least not yet.

We have rented out our house in Bozeman for a year, unfurnished. Doug built a 10 X 12 storage shed in the backyard, and we crammed it full of all our furniture and non-tipi possessions. My days of easily moving in the backseat of my car are gone, but there is a feeling of satisfaction knowing we have reduced our life to 10 X 12. We are apprehensive, and friends and family think we are crazy.

The only one who can't wait to hit the trail is our one-year old mutt, O'Malley. During the past year, we had known that Cisco and Pancho's days on this earth were dwindling. We made two trips to the vet that pierced us to the core. Cisco, the obsessive compulsive stick-fetcher, rock chewer, had ground his teeth down to the gums and stumbled around trance-like. Pancho, always a glutton for comfort, choosing never to exert an ounce of energy unless absolutely necessary, had just given up. He stopped eating, drinking, and didn't move for days. Their times had come, and we bawled knowing what we were about to do. O'Malley, the next canine in line, quickly filled the void. Another black with white chest lab-like mutt, he was born with extreme adventure in his blood. So much so that he deserves a chapter of his own.

May has a history of being an unkind month in Montana. There can be teaser days of brilliant sunshine and resulting welcoming snow melt. Then, you may wake up the next morning to the backlash, the return of winter in all it's fury, with new snow covering up all the ground revealed the previous day. By the end of May, the rivers of Montana flow with evil force when snow pack begins to melt twenty-four hours a day. Banks are overflowing, roads are submerged, basements within the flood plain are terrorized. If you can avoid Montana in May and return when summer is in full bloom, do it. We, however, are acting on our only option.

I stop counting our trips up and down the hill. I just know I am glad when the last pack officially arrives, and we break out the battery-powered radio and a box of wine and reflect on the day's activities. Recounting the walks up, Doug and I have found natural stopping points along the road, and we begin nicknaming these "stages". They eventually become known as the Antlers, Derrick's Landing, the Bog, Flame-Out Bend, and the Boundary. Every time I walk or ski in, I use these benchmarks to track my progress. It also later becomes a way to geographically reference where something occurs, where we saw an animal, or where we caution a warning about road conditions. We routinely incorporate "just before Derrick's Landing" or "at the Antlers" into normal conversation. Code.

The next morning is already a work day. There is no way to sugar-coat the absolute drudgery of peeling logs. It is tedious and grueling work. We unintentionally make it at least twice as difficult on ourselves. In early March, Elroy, the horse logger, fell, hauled and stacked the 50+ de-limbed logs into a huge pile uphill from the cabin site. In yet the first of many "I wish I had known that before" moments, we later learn that there is a best time to harvest and peel logs, and that our timing does not precisely follow the advice of the experts. What cannot be overlooked, however, is that we are here and the logs are here at the same time, and nothing further is going to get done without peeled logs. End of discussion.

The tools of the log peeling trade haven't changed in hundreds of years. For a solid month, my best friend and worst enemy is the drawknife. It is a slightly concave curved hand tool, with one long cutting bevel edge and a wood handle on either end. Straddling a log and grasping the drawknife with both hands, the tool is operated by positioning it at a slight angle to the log and drawing it toward you.

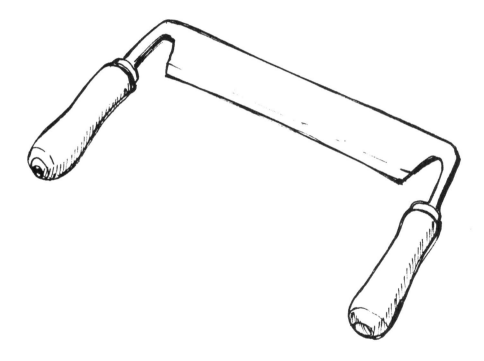

The drawknife

At least, that's the theory. The orneriness of Douglas Fir bark has us blindsided. At the butt end of the logs, the bark was often 4 inches thick. By the tip end, it tapers to perhaps an inch. There is no way any drawknife is going to penetrate a 4 inch fortress. Even after attacking the butt ends of the logs with ax and chainsaw to make headway through the steel-belted bark, we finally hold up the white flag. We claim those ends will be too big to use anyway, and cut them off. Problem solved and firewood pile started.

It makes me realize what a natural defense mechanism thick tree bark is against wildland fire. I am conditioned to seeing the paper-thin bark on Lodgepole Pine in Yellowstone, the omnipresent native tree which burned by the millions during the fires of 1988. Rather than a good defense, the Lodgepole Pine depends on its offense for survival. Its serotinous pine cones only release seeds for regeneration with heat, as during a fire.

In May, the stack of logs is shaded until mid-morning. The nights are still well below freezing at 6300 feet, and at 8:00 in the morning we have to work fast, real fast to generate enough body heat to stay warm. The logs are caked in snow and ice, and I locate scraps of foam rubber to sit on as I straddle and inch my way along.

What I discover, however, is that it doesn't take long before I am peeling off more clothes layers than bark layers. Initially, we have one drawknife, and we take turns. As we form a small pile of peeled logs, Doug gets antsy to start laying sill logs into position on the piers. So, I inherit the job of chief peeler.

In a former life I may have been an assembly worker, always trying to beat my best time. I know that I approach repetitive tasks by trying to streamline the procedure, looking to establish a rhythm and develop time-saving techniques. On a good day, I can peel five logs. There are fewer good days than not-so-good days. I pray to be asked to go into town, or hear Doug yell for help. I curse that the bark peels off in chunks instead of long graceful strips.

As the number of peeled logs increases, I wonder if there is any logic in identifying individual logs for later use. I initiate a very simple but invaluable system. We always carry a little orange grid Park Service notebook in our shirt pockets. With every log I peel, I maintain a numerical index. I mark the number on each log end with a grease pencil, then record the corresponding number in the "logbook", along with overall usable length, butt diameter and tip diameter. As the log courses are going up, if we need a 17 foot log with a 10 inch diameter we can easily look in the book and find the one that most closely matches our needs. The logbook system proves to work perfectly throughout the building phase.

The most critical aspect of peeling logs is having a sharp tool. Even if you have the most expensive tool, if it isn't properly maintained it won't get the job done. And I need all the help I can get. I never quit for the day until I have sharpened the drawknife, ready and waiting for the next morning. One day a friend tells us about a barking spud, an approximately 24 inch wood handle with a narrow steel curved blade that slices under the bark, sort of like a shovel. The friend had never used it but said it came highly recommended. I am already envisioning a miracle product, and ordered one special delivery by day's end from a company in Maine. When it arrives and we experiment according to the instructions, it is less successful than a pocket knife. The bark doesn't budge. We try sharpening the blade until it is like a razor, but nothing changes.

Frustrated, I pack it up, write a letter explaining my disappointment, and return it to the company asking for a refund.

A couple weeks later, a large package arrives in the mail. The barking spud is returned with a rather nasty letter from the president. He indicates that they cannot refund my money because the product has been used and now can't be re-sold. I wait a couple days before calling, thinking about my strategy all the while. None other than the president of the company answers the phone. He remembers my letter and his reply immediately, so I pick up where the letter left off. I indicate that I had full intention of keeping this product if it had fulfilled my needs; that it is impossible for me to know that the product does not work as described unless I have used it; and that I want my money back now. He flat out refuses. Later that day, Doug and I were at our favorite hardware store, the wonderful Owenhouse Hardware in Bozeman, a store that bases its reputation on customer service. Out of the blue we noticed that they carry the very same barking spud manufactured by the same company in Maine. We begin telling them our story, mostly just to vent. Without hesitation, they tell us to bring it in and they will trade us the barking spud for a drawknife. End of story. I want to call that company president back and shout: "Nyah, nyah, nyah, nyah, nyah, nyah." But I don't.

It seems that I am getting better at peeling the logs. Maybe I am, probably I'm not. Day by day, the pile shrinks. The muscles in my forearms begin to resemble Popeye's in girth, but by the end of the day are so inflamed I can barely lift my wine glass. At night when I fall into my sleeping bag, my arms and wrists keep me from falling asleep or wake me up. Only one position allows me to be comfortable. If I lay on my back with arms at my side, elbows bent 90 degrees and hands pointed straight up, the agony subsides. The pain is then replaced by a repeating loop dream, nightmare really, of peeling logs, one at a time.

As if being pardoned by the governor and released from prison, Yellowstone National Park contacts me and offers me a job at the South Entrance Station, where Doug will be returning in less than a week. They ask if I am interested. Am I interested? At that point I will pay them to work there. The last few logs can wait until later.

Nancy, left, and friend Colette, peel some of the first logs. Nancy is ecstatic to have help even if it is for only one or two logs.

During the middle of the summer, Doug's sisters and their families all convene in Montana for a week's vacation outside Livingston, where they rent a house. They all volunteer to work at the cabin, including kids, many whose ages were in single-digits. Doug assigns jobs, matching temperament to task. The teenagers engage in a log peeling contest to see who can produce the longest intact strip of bark. I point out my mound of, at the most, six-inch length chips, give a little instruction on the drawknife and wish them good luck. A short time later, they are whooping and hollering, taking turns standing on the logs holding 10 foot bark strips like they are prize-winning fish. The bark slides off like butter. Amazing what an additional 60 days of sitting in the sun will do. Log peeling has been transformed from agony to ecstasy. I'll never know if this is what the experts meant. "You can observe a lot by just watching" Yogi Berra would have said.

Nancy

10

R–E–S–P–E–C–T

Whenever you are asked if you can do a job, tell 'em, 'Certainly I can!' Then get busy and find out how to do it.

-- Theodore Roosevelt

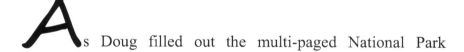

As Doug filled out the multi-paged National Park

Service application, I looked over his shoulder and compared it to taking the SAT test. Page after page of No. 2 lead pencil bubble marks, a self-evaluation of life skills, education and accomplishments. All for an entry-level job at an entrance kiosk. We were so brutally honest when we each filled out our first application, savagely analyzing whether our ability to give a presentation, paddle a canoe or change a typewriter ribbon was really a "3" or "4". We have few, if any, "5s", indicating expert qualification. It isn't until later that another seasonal ranger confided the applicant's mantra, "If you have ever been to a Chinese restaurant, rate your fluency in the Chinese language at least a "3". You then have six months in which to learn. In other words, lie like hell." The competition for Park Service jobs is fierce, and unless your application is infused with lots of 5s, it gets shoved to the back of the pack. Show your moxie!

It seems to me, hiring in the Park Service is a bit like scoring figure skating in the Olympics. If you have been around awhile and paid your dues, you eventually rise to the top of the heap. And working an entrance station is nothing if not paying dues.

Doug's seasonal employment in Yellowstone begins on a sad note. A backcountry ranger died in a kayak accident while on patrol in a freak windstorm, and his girlfriend decided to resign her position and return home. It is the middle of summer 1994, high season in Yellowstone, and someone who can be there yesterday is needed. When Doug receives the call, the offer partially hinges on how soon he can report for duty. "Will noon tomorrow be too late?" he asks. When he calls home several days later to describe his new living accommodations, it sounds like a sitcom. "I'm old enough to be the father of my roommates. I live in the bunkhouse with Missy, Chrissy and Boone," he says. Nonetheless, listening to his tales of life in Yellowstone are alluring, enough so that I apply the summer of 1995 after I resign my position at the university.

The mystique of the National Park Service is riveting, and the mission to "preserve and protect... this pleasuring ground for the people" engages Doug immediately. The actual job at the entrance kiosk, a repetitious "Hello, welcome to Yellowstone", selling entrance passes and handing out park literature, is as boring as it sounds. It is the people you meet through the job that are anything but boring. None are your usual 9-to-5ers. Individually, their interests are all over the map: school teacher, geologist, writer, real estate agent, accountant, linguist, med student, geographer, artist, and the list goes on. As a group, the common thread is helping save these last best places by educating the public about their resources. It's an idea that has worked since 1872, when Yellowstone was established as the first national park, "the mother park".

The South Entrance, the Snake River Ranger Station, is as the name implies, at the south end of Yellowstone. Visitors arrive after driving through Jackson, Wyoming and Teton National Park. I'm sure for some people this is the longest distance they have ever driven between points of civilization. Even though they never leave the road, this is probably wilderness to them. City slickers, more comfortable remaining within the safety of their car or motor home.

At the South Entrance, there are no concessions, no restaurants, no visitor center, no shopping mall, no souvenir shops. With only a vault toilet, a few picnic tables, and the backcountry permit office and ranger station, most visitors buzz through the entrance station to more populated destinations beyond. Others arrive in dust-encrusted Subarus, every square inch packed with outdoor recreational equipment, the hard core wilderness aficionados. National parks attract a cross-section of not only America, but the world. To me, this pastoral setting is idyllic, situated right on the Snake River, away from the bumper-to-bumper tourist traps at Old Faithful or Mammoth. When there are evening sightings of grizzly bears on the river, the employees have the viewing to themselves. At night, only the bugling of bull elk or yipping of coyotes pierce the stillness.

Our lives in and out of Yellowstone dovetail as if hand-crafted for each other. The bounty of animal tracks and scat present in the park offer me hours of field education, from analyzing paw or hoof size and gait to reconstructing their last meal. On my hikes up to the top of the ridge at the cabin property with O'Malley, I follow animal trails. I make note of elk browse on young tree saplings, matted grasses from elk and deer bedding down, hoof tracks splayed by an elk on the run, or a huge pile of fresh steaming bear scat letting me know it was in the neighborhood. Of course, O'Malley is aware of these details long before me, he just keeps it to himself.

One of our duties at the South Entrance is horse wrangler. We groom and feed the horses used in backcountry patrols. Doug is fascinated; he completed a horseshoeing class several years earlier. If he were closer to 20 rather than 50, I could easily imagine him as a backcountry ranger. I grew up amidst oil refineries and steel mills, and I have never been around horses much, and would rather remain outside the corral. I loved watching our horse logger, Elroy, with his two Percheron draft horses, inching 20 foot logs up the snow-covered ravine. He had one of those horses responding as deftly as a circus animal. What would it take to establish that level of comfort?

Dave, the backcountry ranger, takes each seasonal ranger one on one, and gives us painstaking horse care instructions. He carefully assesses our skill level, our "fear-o-meter", and enthusiasm. I know I did not lie on this part on my application. Just because my childhood Saturday mornings included *Roy Rogers* and *The Cisco Kid* does not mean I rate myself a "5" in the horse category. Surprising myself, I grow to love working with the horses, except for the 'fly dope' part, which somehow ended up mostly on me. There is a very specific order to tie up, groom, feed, then release each horse. Seniority rules, even in the horse world and if they are tied up or released in the wrong order, bullying would ensue. They sport such individual personalities, but there is also a group dynamic worthy of an animal behavior research project. Follow the pecking order and all is right with the world. Do it your own way and see what happens. You will get no arguments from me in this regard.

Doug and I work a long season, until the end of October. The roads close after the first significant snow in November, allowing a base to accumulate and later re-open for snowmobiles. We wish the last "Welcome to Yellowstone" of the year and board up the kiosk. All the other seasonals have long since scattered, shifting back to school or other national parks with extended seasons. Only die-hard visitors enter the park at this time. Even developed areas like Old Faithful or Lake Village are ghost towns. Early in October, Dave approaches Doug and me with an offer to horsepack into the Harebell and Fox Creek cabins, a five-day trip. Before I even speak, Doug accepts for us. But grooming and feeding are one thing, at least my feet are firmly planted on the ground. This is no longer a level playing field.

Without me voicing my trepidation, Dave senses it and assigns me Harvey, the most steadfast trail-wise horse of the string. Harvey doesn't spook, Harvey doesn't bolt, I just have to sit on his back. While this knowledge calms my nerves somewhat, the view from several feet up in the saddle rekindles it quickly. Nineteen miles the first day, my knees in a death grip around Harvey, I am peeled out of the saddle just in time to collapse. At camp that night, the others recount spectacular vistas along the trail. All I remember is the short expanse from the back of Harvey's head to six feet in front of him. Each day I gain a little confidence, experimenting turning in the saddle or attempting talking and riding at the same time. By the last day I must look downright equestrian. As we ready to cross the Snake River on our return to the Ranger Station, Dave hands me the lead rope for the pack string and instructs me how to guide them across the river. The panic that sets in is both visible and audible, but Dave doesn't back down. I know that Harvey can do it, and I convince myself that either Dave has enough confidence in me or a good backup plan, or both. So I head down the bank and into the river, pack string following behind me. The current pushes us downstream just as Dave has said and I work against it, focusing straight across to the opposite bank. At that moment, mountain man Jim Bridger and I are soul mates.

During my nearly 10 years' seasonal employment in Yellowstone, I am a sponge, immersing myself in the "place" and sopping up every experience provided. Welcoming visitors to Yellowstone was the tip of the iceberg, and I am hooked after one season. The following five summers, I discover a niche in the Division of Interpretation, stationed at the Grant Visitor Center. Evening campfire slide programs and geyser basin walks, as well as choreographing visitors' travel plans, the weeks fly by. Well into the night I research Yellowstone, its geology, history, flora and fauna, with the hope of legitimately responding to visitors' demands for answers. The variety of questions I am asked is directly proportional to the number of visitors I encounter each day. I always feel I need to stay one step ahead of them. I become a student of animal behavior, geology, fire ecology, drought, and natural resources. I renew my love of hiking, heading out before and after my shift. Sharing those personal trail experiences, passing along tips about where to see animals or birds, heightens visitor contact. When those same individuals return to the Visitor Center to recount their adventure, it enables me to see things through new eyes.

What may leave the greatest impression on a Park Service employee, in my opinion, is wearing the uniform, the green and gray. And, more precisely, the flat hat, commonly called the Smokey the Bear hat. Put on the uniform and you suddenly find yourself on a pedestal. While there are very few physical specimens that actually look good wearing the uniform, nearly everyone's psyche assumes that they do. Rangers in flat hats are akin to the Pied Piper of Hamelin, minus the musical instrument. The hat commands R-E-S-P-E-C-T. Thanks, Aretha.

What I learn in Yellowstone accompanies me to the cabin, and what I learn at the cabin works its way into my jobs in Yellowstone. Geographically, our cabin is within the greater Yellowstone ecosystem, and, like the television commercial advocates "The more you know, the more you want to know." For me, the puzzle pieces are suddenly fitting together and I want to be able to help visitors understand the connections. In Yellowstone, millions of dead burned trees are still standing, sentinels remaining from the Fires of '88. Even 10 years later, angry visitors storm into the Visitor Center, demanding to know why we let this "destruction, devastation, and damage" occur. We say we can see the "D" words on their lips as they come through the door. I feel we owe them the information that allows them to understand and reach their own conclusion. All the right conditions existed in 1988 for Yellowstone to go up in smoke that summer: it was the driest winter on record, the wettest spring on record, no summer precipitation accompanied by dry lightning strikes, and decades of fire suppression resulting in a build-up of fuel on the forest floor. What most visitors have heard about is the so-called "Let It Burn" policy, not the fact that the forests didn't die, that forests have been burning for thousands of years, that Native Americans intentionally set fires, that fire rejuvenates a forest.

The afternoon Doug and I stand alongside the road watching the fire creep up the ridge toward our property and cabin, I keep reminding myself of all the fire ecology benefits. We had looked around and taken absolutely nothing with us, even though there was time to gather up treasured possessions. "It's just stuff" we said, "just stuff".

I love the mission of the Park Service, but I am probably not a good fit for government protocol. "Too much of a rebel," is probably written somewhere in my personnel file. I'd rather it say "rebel with a cause". I speak my mind, an individual quality not always appreciated in large organizations. Early in 2000, a position for a naturalist/guide at the Yellowstone Association Institute is advertised, and I imagine it being created with me in mind. YAI, the educational arm of Yellowstone Association, does not necessarily solicit rebels, but does operate outside a government framework. As an instructor, it is assumed that I know what I am doing, and if I have a problem I know who to contact. It is a novel concept that I feel should be replicated. As an Institute naturalist/guide, I teach five day field classes to a maximum 12 students, a sort of Intro to Yellowstone 101. I teach on the trail as we hike in summer, and as we ski and snowshoe in winter. The beauty of the program is that students don't just learn, they experience through participation. Our classroom is always in the field, where my props are readily at hand and visual aids are the real thing. Sleuthing animal tracks, dissecting scat, feeling tiny gnaw marks on antlers, even discerning the difference between a flat Doug Fir needle and a multi-sided Englemann Spruce needle---how can these be better accomplished in a book? What the students take away from these classes is the real thing. It is the knowledge that they have been there, done that.

From the moment I pick up students in early morning, until I drop them off at the hotel in late afternoon, we bond. They are generally middle-aged, well-educated and well-traveled, and hungry for knowledge about Yellowstone. That's why they are taking a class rather than sight-seeing on their own. They challenge me and bombard me with questions. On a good day, I can answer some; most days I return to my room to do research. In the winter, we travel from venue to venue via snowcoach, a 12-passenger van converted to an over-snow track vehicle. We putt along at 20 miles per hour, so there is lots of time to fill. I tell stories about my favorite historical characters in Yellowstone or we discuss the hot topics of wolf reintroduction or bison and brucellosis. Milepost by milepost, we become intimate with the thermal features and charismatic megafauna of Yellowstone. I make a point of steering clear of politics and religion.

My students always want to know more about me and what my life outside of the park is like. Once, I mention that I like working in Yellowstone in winter because I have electricity and indoor plumbing. That little comment doesn't just slip by and they hold me hostage until I tell them about the tipi and cabin. The rest of the trip they equate me to some of Yellowstone's nineteenth century explorers. "Whoa!" I think, these folks must really have a limited definition of "roughing it".

"Change is the only constant," accurately describes the dynamic nature of Yellowstone National Park. Thermal features undergo abrupt or imperceptible transformations, shifting their activity levels to the consternation or delight of expectant visitors. Overnight sensations or overnight duds, their fame rises and falls like politicians. So mesmerizing are the geysers, hot pools and mud pots that a pilgrimage of three and a half million people flock to Yellowstone each year. Their crusade is not only for the thermal features, but the charismatic megafauna, wolves, grizzly bears, bison, elk.

Tourist season in Yellowstone resembles a bell curve, May and September are the legs and July the apex. Visitors begin to trickle into the park as roads and facilities open in May, intrepid travelers not put off by snow-packed trails or few services. By July, a three-ring circus unfolds. Hulking motor homes crawl up the switch-backed Dunraven Pass in an aluminum procession. Throngs of people are plastered like ants on the Old Faithful boardwalk. They sip sodas, crunch chips and ready handfuls of cameras in anticipation of the geyser's eruption. "Animal jams" in the Hayden Valley, miles-long vehicle clogs caused by a herd of bison crossing the road or a grizzly feeding on a carcass, shut down traffic for hours. With no shoulders on the roads, visitors just stop and fling car doors open and run off in desperate pursuit of photographs.

My early-season excitement is long gone by July and I ache for September when the crowds thin. Each returning year I notice that I arrive at my tipping point a little sooner. I am not as accepting of change as Mother Nature is, especially when I see those changes threatening nature itself. Hordes of people descending upon the park like a plague of locusts are impacting not only the natural resources, but the quality of the experience. A mile away from the road on the trail, it is bliss; It's the law of diminishing backcountry pedestrians. "Welcome to Yellowstone" is disappearing from my vocabulary.

Nancy

11

NPR AND A FIVE LITER WINEBOX

If you remain in your comfort zone you will not go any further.

– Catherine Pulsifer

We were a carload of Extension Service employees, bored, driving across Montana from Bozeman to Ekalaka to conduct outreach training. Over the 400 mile road trip, we rotated through conversational topics like cards on a Rolodex. The current subject was giving personal definition to "roughing it", a common enough expression heard in Montana. One response---a warm beer and a black and white TV---made me howl. Little did I know that within a few years, I'd be bargaining with the devil for either.

Doug and I think of ourselves as normal. It has never been our intention to abandon the comforts of civilization while building the cabin. We appreciate plumbing and running water and being safe from inclement weather. That being said, we have proven to ourselves that in order to make any real and sustained progress in building the cabin, it is imperative we live on site. As we see it, options are few. Even under the best of conditions, there is no way a temporary trailer can make it up the switchbacks. Nor could we or would we consider hiring a contractor. A thin bank account addresses the 'could' part of the equation, and our dream of being our own builders buttonholes the 'would'. We have the tipi, we have the camping gear, and perhaps most importantly, we have the passion. Our life in the woods begins.

Little by little, more out of necessity than objective, our temporary living compound organically evolves. We have thought little beyond knowing we will sleep in the tipi and use the outhouse for 'facilities'. Now, instead of just arriving and working for several hours before leaving, suddenly this camp is home, at least until the cabin is livable. If we can't make it cozy, it should at least be habitable. It is like an HGTV design challenge. From the cabin site to the tipi is approximately one city block. Along the winding path connecting the most distant structures are the cook shed, outhouse and summer patio. I think of our multiple living spaces as zones, and definitely not in an Architectural Digest sort of way, but more because they are distinct areas. The selection of the cabin site merits significant discussion, assessment of sunrise/sunset patterns, and a nod to the best view on the most level ground. The temporary structures are erected wherever there is a clearing in the trees and a quasi-level piece of ground. No point in getting too comfortable.

The first order of design intervention is creating a kitchen. A severe lack of take-out restaurants at the end of our road implies that we will be eating in. I clear out the 6 X 8 tool shed Doug built, converting it into a cook shed. The tools don't need locking up anymore, except when we leave for extended periods. I recruit Doug to build a narrow right-angle plywood countertop for workspace, cookstove, and dishpan. This cuts down on the already scant floor space in the shed, but any half-decent chef will tell you they can't cook without counter space. I transform the exposed studs of the uninsulated walls into plate and utensil racks with little scraps and slats of wood. A cup rack is another wood slat with angled nails as hooks. So bloody simple, relatively mouse-proof, and tidy. Lidded plastic food bins and five-gallon water buckets occupy the sacrificed floor space under the counters and provide pull-out seating for Doug while I am cooking.

For my entire adult life I have been schlepping around my parents' 40 year old Coleman two-burner cookstove and lantern, using them car camping. Now they have a permanent home. Coleman stoves from the 1950s require initial and continuous pumping of the white gas fuel tank while cooking. After running the chainsaw and pounding nails all day, Doug is not in the mood to pump a fuel tank for an hour while the old Coleman sputters weakly and I stir the pot. We upgrade to something slightly less vintage, a cast iron, propane fired two burner.

Everything we pack away, hang up, or leave out is done so with the relentless mouse population in mind. Given time, mice will eventually chew their way through anything. It is humiliating to be so easily outwitted. We wage an endless battle against their heroic efforts. They are brazen, unceasingly taunting us, performing well-choreographed routines across the countertop in full view. During one eventful meal preparation, a pounding sound startles me. When I turn around, Doug has proudly speared a mouse on the end of the long-handled BBQ fork. Not in any hurry to repeat the BBQ scene from Farley Mowat's Never Cry Wolf, he immediately flings it into the trash. Although I loath the dim lighting conditions in the cook shed, an off-white Coleman lantern hissing glow, I am at least grateful not to know just how many dog hairs and mouse turds we actually consume in any given meal. The only real culinary weapon we have against the mice is a rusty non-working avocado hued refrigerator. It leans somewhat precariously behind the cook shed in a continuously shady spot. The refrigerator's previous owner thought us off our rockers to take it off his hands so willingly. We scavenge usable materials from its innards and re-purpose it into a seasonal mouse-proof cupboard. In the winter, it serves as a reliable freezer while during the summer, with a block or two of ice, it keeps lettuce edible for a few days and a 12-pack of beer not quite cold. The only things missing are a few good magnets.

During the summer, we rarely need flashlights or headlamps outdoors. In Montana, it stays light late. On full moon nights, once you adjust, you can walk through the woods at a pretty good clip just using your own peepers. Honest. Inside the cook shed and tipi we depend on oil and kerosene lamps with wicks, and a Coleman lantern and Aladdin oil lamp that uses knit fabric mantles. Oil lamps with tall glass chimneys and wicks haven't changed much since pioneer days. They cast a nice glow, but if you are trying to do anything that requires sight, forget it. The wicks need regular trimming or the flame burns erratically and smudges the chimney. Mantle lighting is a definite improvement in terms of candle-power, but once the mantles have been used even once they become fragile. A bump to the chimney, or in our case, the persistent buzzing of hundreds of kamikaze miller moths, leads to sudden and inevitable mantle death.

Improvements in our daily living situation are usually the result of repetitions of, "Man, I wish I had _____". It might be a place to sit, a place to hang something, or the goal to reduce a few steps going back and forth between living zones. Whatever it is, the solution is always simple and out of materials on hand. And usually constructed on the spot with instant gratification.

We move into our new digs at the tipi in early May 1995. Although summer in Montana is still more than a month away, we know we will be spending increasingly more time outside. We have a few wooden pallets, courtesy of the local newspaper office, some severely damaged plywood, and within 30 minutes an outdoor pallet patio materializes. Add a couple of weathered Adirondack chairs, a spool table, and we are ready for visitors, almost. The few and daring that do come eye us for signs of mental breakdown. Next to the pallet patio we dig a fire pit, and this relaxing spot competes with memories of our lush, green Bozeman back yard. With good NPR reception and a five-liter wine box close at hand, life is as good as it gets. O'Malley provides constant entertainment hunting critters of varying species. After awhile I head back to the cook shed and

plunge into dinner preparations, usually one-pot delicacies, for simplicity's sake.

The casual observer may too easily assume that we are not concerned about cleanliness or hygiene. As much as it is earthly possible, we are. It isn't easy, and other than each other there really is no one to impress. When we are working in Yellowstone and only weekending at the cabin, we save our hygiene routine for our government quarters, 170 miles away. But on the day our seasonal contract ends, so does the running water and laundry facilities. The outhouse, as has been described, is flawless in its function and design. It is private, odor-free, and as long as the toilet paper is suspended there is little evidence of mice. The magazine rack is a nice touch, although the choice of reading material is limited: an eclectic mixture of *High Country News*, *Time Magazine* and *This Old House*. After a summer visit by Doug's family, a few *National Enquirers* mysteriously appear. The outhouse is neither heated nor insulated, so during the winter you don't want to linger any longer than necessary. Character-building, some might say. Toothbrushes, toothpaste and floss are kept in the cook shed, where we also have a pocket mirror and maybe a comb or brush. That about does it for articles of beautification.

Figuring out how to successfully shower outside is a trial, especially in winter. Winter compounds the level of difficulty of nearly everything. Showering requires water, and water, at this point, has to be hauled in on the supply sled behind the snowmobile in winter. Any water wasted is water that is not easily replaced. We do try to limit our trips into town for supplies in winter, as it usually blows a day, but we never return without water. If we run out of drinking water between town days, we melt snow until it boils and filter it through paper coffee filters to remove the big chunks. I guess the fact that we continue to survive is testimony to the high filtration ability of mere paper. I'm not testifying to the taste of paper-filtered water, just the relative non-toxicity.

We have an old Sun Shower, the water-filled black plastic bladder that sits in the sun until the water heats up, but it is totally inadequate in winter. It we are lucky, it reaches a temperature frat boys might use during initiation hazing pranks. Showers are minimalist: rinse, lather, rinse, consuming as little water as possible. Later, we advance to a twentieth century version of the Sun Shower; this one heats the water with a small propane tank. Guaranteed hot water, but no guarantee against a cool breeze. We never take the time to construct a shower enclosure, because we always intend to do something more permanent once the cabin is complete.

Whenever we make a trip over the hill to Bozeman, we stop to see old friends. I'm sure they interpret our visit purely as an opportunity to use their indoor plumbing; our towels always seem too quick to appear. One friend finally suggests that we split his $60 a month office rental, where the conference room includes a bathroom with shower. We leave a bag with clean clothes and a few books in the office, and hang out there just long enough to take a shower. We always seem to have the place to ourselves. This scheme runs smoothly for several months until exiting from the bathroom one afternoon, an impromptu meeting of several non-profit directors is convened in the conference room. We make our entrance with towels and toiletries in hand, looking as bizarre as Kramer making an entrance in *Seinfeld*. We politely greet the eyes now focusing on us and just keep on walking. The next day, the building landlord asks us to leave.

Our next and final showering station, until the cabin is complete, is the truck stop in Livingston. Long-haul truckers like to feel refreshed on the road, and truck stops oblige. Two showers for five bucks, we walk through the aisles of mudflaps and NASCAR decals just like all the real truckers on our regular cleansing pilgrimages. Then, as a special treat, we go out for lunch on the one day a week we look presentable. As a real indulgence, we choose not to eat at the truck stop.

At the opposite ends of our compound, the tipi is not visible from the cabin site. We pitch it on higher ground than the cabin in a small clearing. Since hardly a flat place to stand exists on our property, we spend a day leveling out about a 20 foot diameter circle. We want the tipi door to face east, as is the common practice in Native American cultures, to welcome the morning sun. The choice of directions is in our favor, as east is the low side of the now-leveled pad. The rear of the tipi will butt up against an 8 inch dirt retaining wall.

We have been camping out in the tipi for more than a year, throwing sleeping bags and Therma-rest pads on the ground. I patched the bear claw rips in the canvas, and the one remaining paw print is hardly visible. We leave the tipi door rolled up, so any curious animal is free to investigate without tearing through the wall. After several days peeling logs, hoisting logs, cranking logs, and cursing logs, sleeping on the ground gets harder and harder. Getting

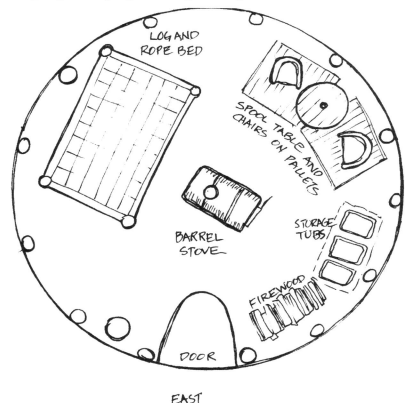

EAST

up off the ground becomes increasingly more difficult. Doug takes a few hours off to build a primitive log pole bed with a nylon rope suspension system woven back and forth through holes drilled into the logs. As far as I am concerned, a Tempur-Pedic mattress wouldn't be any better.

We don't need much in the way of clothes. Work clothes and town clothes are stored in plastic tubs, just in case mice might want to try some on. Town clothes are put on after a shower or when going out for lunch. Work clothes are for everything else. We follow old pioneer logic, everyday clothes and Sunday-go-to-meetin' clothes. Inside an 18 foot tipi, there is a surprising amount of room. With the bed on one side, we fashion a sitting area opposite it. We visit the newspaper office for a few more pallets, our storage locker for plastic lawn chairs, spool table, oil lamp and rugs, and retreat within the tipi after dinner in the colder months. We read until bedtime, an hour too early to admit, close the tipi door, and crash. A few too many trips in the middle of a winter night getting dressed and traipsing to the outhouse precipitates designating a five-gallon bucket as a chamber pot. O'Malley is able to hold it all night, and curls up on a thick pile of rugs.

I am always charmed to enter the tipi and see the decorated lining. A group of twenty-eight kids at the museum painted handprints and symbols on the lining canvas in primary colors. Kids being kids, the results are all over the map. Some actually looked like hands, others more like cave paintings. Nevertheless, it is always a cheery sight especially on a nasty winter day.

Part of our daily winter routine is stacking firewood in the tipi for the barrel stove. It consumes wood faster than O'Malley does food. It is a 30 gallon drum converted into a very basic heating unit with a stove pipe rising up to the apex of the tipi. Native American cultures, historically, had open fires in their tipis, and we did give that a try. The smoke flaps of the tipi are designed to control and disperse smoke from a fire, but trust me, it is inevitable that campfire smoke permeates everything including human tissue, inside and out. Look at old photos of Native Americans and their weathered faces. The barrel stove doesn't have the ambiance of a campfire, but perhaps I won't have leathery skin and emphysema either. When it is fully stoked, it cranks out the heat unmercifully, causing us to peel layers off like an onion. As the stove cools, we can't get the layers on again fast enough. It is always one or the other.

There is a woodstove etiquette procedure followed in the National Park Service backcountry cabins that has no doubt saved a few rangers' lives. Before you depart from a backcountry cabin, you lay a fire for the next ranger arriving. That ranger might be injured or transporting someone injured, or have been lost on the trail in a blizzard. All they have to do is strike the matches setting on top of the stove to the properly stacked paper and kindling and a fire will be blazing in no time. It is the unwritten code, one well appreciated, and if ever forgotten is only forgotten once. Although we honor this code, at the tipi there is no one to enforce it, and we tend to ignore it.

At first, the tipi is dramatic, elegant, graceful, even majestic. By the end, it is shabby, wretched, pathetic, barely standing. The canvas, which was donated to my internship project, turned out not to be UV protected. Hard to cry foul over something that is free. Where the canvas is covered by coats of latex paint, the fabric is strong and impervious to rain, snow and sun. It is where it is not painted that it suffers miserably. The upper third of the tipi is a golden yellow, the sun; the middle third unpainted white canvas with royal blue hailstones raining down; the bottom third is totally unpainted canvas.

As winter progresses, snow piles up around the exterior, drifts grow higher and higher. On one hand, it creates a layer of insulation that is most welcome on the inside. It also pushes against a weakening fabric, which starts to rip. Then it starts to rot the fabric. Once the drifts reach the hailstones, they start popping out like shooting stars, the fabric rotting away around them. Duct tape saves the day, and the inside of the tipi starts to look like an Airstream trailer, such is the metallic reflection in the light of the oil lamps. We tape over each hailstone and fabric rip. On the outside, the snow drifts are hard pack and cemented there until spring, so we follow the artist Christo's lead and wrap the tipi in brown tarps. We then christen it the "tarpi". On the day we move into the cabin, we allow the tarpi to die with dignity and strip it down from the poles. The painted design became its greatest weakness. Too late, I realize, if I had painted the entire canvas, it would still be standing.

The cook shed

Doug

12

MRS. FLICKINGER'S SIX
SIMPLE MACHINES

*If you can't explain it to a six year old, you don't understand it
yourself.*

--Albert Einstein

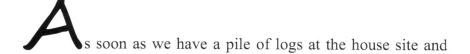

s soon as we have a pile of logs at the house site and

peel one or two, I can see we have a major problem. The logs are
green, full of moisture and have a layer of heavy bark. It is
tremendous work to move them anywhere at all. We move the first
two logs with a come-along and some aircraft cable with hooks
attached. It works well enough for moving them from one pile to
another, but getting them from the peeled pile to the deck of the
cabin? It's not going to work. We need a new idea.

In the old days, settlers were generally blessed with a flat spot to build. They could place a couple of smaller logs as inclined planes, from the ground to the wall, and use their horse or an ox, or mechanical advantage to roll the logs onto the wall. Other solutions were a gin pole; a tall pole in the center of the cabin, probably set into the ground with guy wires stabilizing it. With a pulley and ropes, and the aforementioned inclined plane, logs could be muscled into place. Of course, by the mid-1990s, a crane mounted on a truck made those methods obsolete.

But, the terrain makes most of those methods impossible at our cabin site. We cannot afford to rent a crane for the entire summer, or one to arrive each time we need to place a log. Like Archimedes who said about his lever, "Give me someplace to stand and I can move the world," there is no place for the crane to operate. Even if there was a place to set up the crane, the access up our road makes its arrival almost impossible. In any case, we're determined to do this as inexpensively as possible. But the inclined plane method with the mechanical advantage of a winch or come-along might work so I file it away in the back of my mind as Plan B.

Do you remember third grade? That was when Mrs. Flickinger taught me and my classmates about the six simple machines; the lever, the wheel and axle, the pulley, the inclined plane, the wedge and screw. During the construction of this cabin, I've already used the lever to muscle logs around, and the wedge to persuade a tree to fall in the right direction. We're about to make creative use of the wheel and axle, the pulley and the screw (or lag bolts, anyway). Thanks Mrs. Flickinger, you'd be proud.

Plan A has come to me in my sleep. I can't guarantee that I haven't seen something like this idea before, but when I look for it in my books, it's nowhere to be found. I may have invented it and if such is the case, you may use it free of charge, I have not patented it. You're welcome to it.

I draw a picture of my invention and show it to a couple of smart, mechanically inclined friends of mine. One is skeptical, the other can't find any reason why it wouldn't work, but wishes me a sarcastic "Good luck".

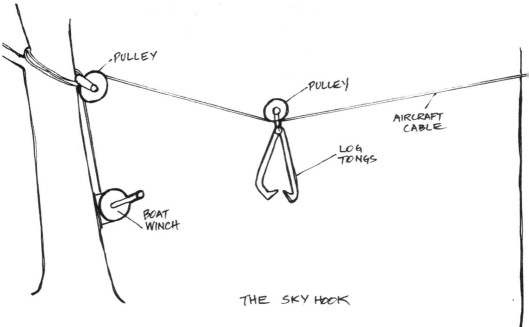

THE SKY HOOK

We have a log carrier, which consists of a stout handle with a set of long tongs dangling from it. With this contraption two people can carry a small log or drag an even bigger one. With two log carriers and four stout men, you can move logs with a bit of effort. But it's just Nancy and me. When we try to use it, with the log acting as a fulcrum, my 260 pounds just tends to push and pull Nancy's 120 pounds around. The log carrier is useless to us, but I have a plan for the log tongs so I disassemble the log carrier. I've bought about 50 yards of aircraft cable and a couple of pulleys, some cable clamps, and a heavy boat winch. Then, I have to make a trip into Livingston and find a metal fabrication shop that will make me a steel bracket so that I can attach the winch to a tree.

Meanwhile, back at the cabin site, I construct a ladder out of two 16 foot 2x4s. I lean the ladder against the largest tree on the uphill side of the cabin site and climb the ladder cutting off a few errant limbs as I go. I attach a pulley as high up as I can reach, approximately 22 feet off the ground; I use five or six feet of aircraft cable and some cable clamps with a couple of loops around the tree.

I haul the unwieldy ladder to the downhill side of the cabin site, cursing its length and weight. On this side of the site, there is no outstanding candidate for hooking onto. I pick a small, but tall tree and attach my cable. I attach that tree to another tree, and the second tree to a third tree, pulling the cable as taut as possible, the theory being--the three trees will act as one.

I drive down to Livingston and pick up my new bracket. I had thoughtfully provided them with a full-scale drawing and it matches exactly, proper 90 degree angle and all the holes in just the right place. After a visit to the hardware store I head back to the cabin site. With a couple huge lag bolts I attach the bracket to the tree and then with some nuts and bolts, the winch to the bracket. The cable stretches from the three trees across the cabin site to the pulley attached to the big tree and down to the winch. The other pulley hangs in the middle, over the cabin site, with the log tongs attached.

The theory is: I crank on the winch and begin to take up slack on the cable, the log tongs grasp the log and as I crank harder the log should rise into the air. In theory, anyway.

I find the smallest of all the logs and with a hammer tap the log tongs through the bark until they bite into the green wood. I walk back to the tree and begin cranking. The cable tightens up, the winch becomes rather hard to crank. I wish I'd gotten heavier cables, winches and pulleys. I look at the cable and all the attachments and wonder if everything will hold together. The three trees tied together bend slightly toward the cabin, and then "Eureka"-- the log begins to rise. As it breaks free from the pile, it begins to move downhill toward the cabin. I can't back off the winch because of its ratcheted mechanism, so the small log smacks into the sill logs with a mighty thunk. But I've done it. I've moved a log, however small, by myself. I need a few refinements, like a come-along and some more cable to control the effect of gravity.

But, hallelujah and praise be to Allah, the "skyhook" is going to work.

Over time we learn that the skyhook is far from perfect, but it will do what it was designed to do and more. Not only will it move logs to the cabin deck, but it will move logs from the unpeeled pile to the peeled pile. With a little help from gravity it will move them downhill, or with the come-along it will move them uphill; we're in business. At first we have trouble moving the bigger and longer logs, but the contraption doesn't break. We find we can maneuver the logs around if we can just get some of the weight onto the skyhook. It doesn't actually have to lift the logs high into the air. And as an added bonus, when the logs are peeled and the weight of the bark is gone, we can deal with all but the heaviest logs. And wonder of wonders, with the bark off, the logs begin to dry out and lose moisture, and therefore weight, at an astonishing speed.

With a little practice, we become rather adept at moving the logs where we want them. Pile to pile or up on the deck to become part of a wall, we've got it down now. It requires a lot of foot traffic, running from the tree with the winch, to the log, to the come-along to the cabin deck and all over again, but it works.

As the summer wears on we find we can do one course of logs, all the way around the cabin in about a weekend, which for us is Wednesday and Thursday. Toward the end of the summer the walls have risen to five or six feet high. The skyhook then begins to falter, but only because I can't make the cable perfectly taut. The slack in the cable becomes more of a problem as each course of logs is added. Finally we just can't muscle the logs any higher. We need more mechanical advantage. But how? With what?

I consult my cabin building library. In Monte Burch's book Building Log Homes I find a picture of a truck mounted crane. It's not too big but, evidently, it does the job. I get out my paper and pencils and begin drawing up some kind of crane that I can build on the deck in the interior of the cabin to help lift the logs just a few feet higher. I draw up another contraption that we call the "Rocket Launcher" because that's what it ends up looking like.

I drive old Rusty down to Livingston and buy about eight 2x6s of various lengths. (They will eventually find themselves used as rafters in about a month and a half.) I buy another boat winch, some lag bolts and some long and heavy nuts and bolts. I also get a kind of wheel device for the cable to ride on without kinking. Up at the cabin site, on the deck, I start to construct a small crane. Two 2x6s form the arm, and two more form the legs, two more act as supports for the legs to keep them from moving around. One more 2x6 keeps the legs from splaying out under the weight. I tack it together with 16 penny nails and then cinch it up with lag bolts and nuts and bolts. Nancy and I attach the winch, the wheel and the cable and hook. We find it's quite heavy, wheels would have been nice, and the next time I have to build a rocket launcher, it will have them. But, nonetheless, it can be moved around on the plywood deck with a little bit of effort.

We try it out for the first time on the log that is hung up that we couldn't get onto the wall. We move the rocket launcher into place, and put the cable and hook around the log. Nancy straddles the rocket launcher while I run over to the tree to the 'controls' of the skyhook and we both fire up our machines and crank away. The log starts to move into place but I hear Nancy screaming "bloody murder" and stop to go investigate. Her 120 pounds is not quite enough ballast and she finds herself on a teeter-totter, about to be launched by the rocket launcher.

We look around the site for more ballast and find the perfect butt end of a log to secure to the tail end. Now we're in business and we soon discover that we should have built this rocket launcher much sooner. We find it a whole lot easier to position the logs to scribe the notches and move the logs back into place after cutting the notches. It is a marvelous addition to our big tool box. But we should have put it on wheels.

The Rocket Launcher being moved into position.

Doug

13

THE TORTOISE NOT THE RABBIT

It doesn't matter how slowly you go as long as you do not stop.

-- Confucius

Late Spring of 1995 finds Nancy and me employed at the

South Entrance of Yellowstone National Park. Our boss has arranged our schedule so that we are both done in the mid-afternoon on Tuesday and don't have to be back until one of our shifts starts at 10 am on Friday. Consequently, Nancy, O'Malley and I are in old Rusty and heading the 180 miles up to Livingston.

We stop in Livingston for groceries, ice, beer, wine and our mail, then head another 15 miles on up to the land. We generally arrive in time to make some sandwiches for dinner and crawl into the tipi until morning. As a rule, we awake to the sun peeking in the tipi door. Naturally, we erected it Sioux fashion, with the door pointing east.

After breakfast our work day begins. We quickly settle into a routine that lasts all summer long. Nancy, poor soul, resumes peeling logs. Before our jobs in Yellowstone began we spent about three weeks constructing the skyhook and then peeling logs together. We had peeled our way through perhaps three quarters of the pile.

The first week of June, after all the snow is gone, the lumberyard in Livingston brings me a load of lumber in their six wheel drive flatbed dump truck, right to the building site. I have ordered floor joists and the plywood sub floor. Compared to the drudgery of peeling logs, it is fairly quick work to attach the joists to the sill logs and then install the floor. Now, I have to saw two logs in half, lengthwise. The north and south sides of the cabin will each begin with a half-log, while the east and west sides will start with a full round log. It's not an easy task to split a log under any circumstances and it is made much harder by my troublesome and ancient Jonsereds chain saw.

I begin an epic struggle with the saw. It stalls and quits, runs poorly and loses power when it's not in an upright position. It shouldn't be this difficult and my temper is about to blow. I saw awhile, stop and jam a wedge into the saw kerf to keep from pinching the sawbar. Another foot, another wedge, another round of pulling out the stalled saw and restarting it. Finally, after struggling to split the shorter of the two logs, I reach my boiling point. I pull the saw from the log and walk over to a stout fir tree. With Nancy watching in silent open-mouthed horror, screaming curses, I raise the saw over my head with both hands and hurl it with all my might into the trunk of the fir tree. The Jonsereds is dead.

We drive into Bozeman to the saw shop and after looking at some used saws, purchase a brand new Husqvarna. Once we tell the salesman what we are doing, he offers to give us a good deal on a Log Wizard. It's a device that attaches to the end of the sawbar, is driven by the saw chain, and basically turns a chainsaw into a gas powered planer. The beauty of the Log Wizard is that it will become very easy to form the saddle notches in the logs. It will also peel bark and flatten the stubs of limbs that still remain on the log. It's too good of a deal to pass up.

The next day we gas up the new Husqvarna and I power through the process of halving the logs in about an hour. The new saw is lighter, more powerful, starts easier and runs cooler than the ancient Jonsereds. I'm very happy. I put the Log Wizard onto the saw and plane the newly cut surface of the half-logs until they are smooth. In no time at all I have the half-logs positioned on the deck and secure them into place by driving some large spikes through the logs, plywood and into the sill logs.

Next, I consult the 'logbook' and find a suitable log. Nancy and I are about to cut our first saddle notch and put down the first full log in the cabin wall. I have consulted Monte Burch's <u>Complete Guide to Building Log Homes</u> and I've learned how it's done. With our skyhook, we set the log we've chosen on top of the half-logs in its close-to-final position. With scraps of wood, I've made a log scriber, basically a giant compass, much like small ones designed for

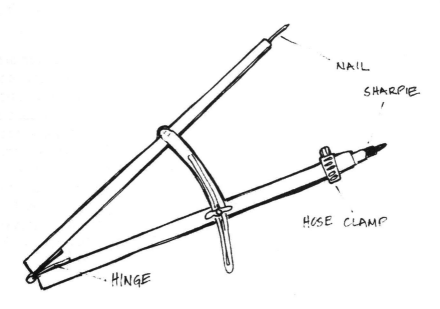

drawing circles. I've built mine out of two 1x1 sticks, a hinge, a nail, a Sharpie and a hose clamp. With the scriber set at about 2-1/2 inches, I trace the shape of the lower log onto the log sitting on top of it. I do it on each side. Then I roll the log over and continue the arcs until I have an oval shape marked on the log.

This is the wood I must remove from the log for it to sit nicely on the log beneath it. I begin by making a series of saw kerfs down to the line I've drawn. Nancy watches the far side so I don't saw too deep. Then we knock out the extraneous wood, first with the hammer end of the hatchet and then a chisel. I finish it off with the log wizard until it's clean and smooth. We've cut our first saddle notch. We cut the notch on the other end of the log in the same fashion and roll the log into place to see how they fit. Well, to be honest, they could be better. We mark the log, make a series of adjustments and fit it again. It's not great but it's serviceable. We'll get better.

We put down a layer of fiberglass insulation on the logs where the notch will sit, to keep air from whistling through the tiny gaps, and roll our notched log into place. We make minor adjustments and drive spikes to attach it to the deck and the logs beneath it. Our first full log is now in place.

Earlier on, I had constructed door and window bucks to the size of our door and window groupings. These are made from 2x8s and 1x3s. I have secured the two door bucks in place at the location of the doors. They have 2x4 bracing holding them upright and plumb. The bucks all have a 1x3 spline dadoed into the uprights; the reason for this is that we are building with green wood. Our logs will continue to lose moisture for two years or so. And while they are losing moisture, they are losing a little bit of their girth, each log shrinking ¾ of an inch. Therefore the log walls will eventually lose about six or seven inches of total height. The spline which matches up with a kerf in the log end allows the logs to settle but still be firmly attached to the door buck.

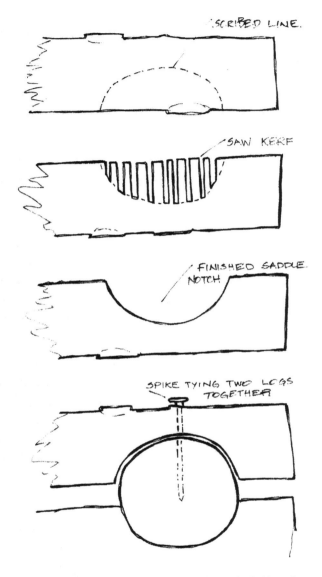

The walls go up, but the progress is painfully slow. Peeling the bark, moving the logs into position, cutting the notches, cutting the kerfs for the door and window bucks, spiking them into place; everything takes an inordinate amount of time. As the walls grow higher most tasks take longer than they did before. Spiking the logs to themselves, for instance, is fairly easy at the height of my knees, but it gets progressively more difficult as we begin working from a ladder. Cutting the notches while standing on the deck is time consuming enough, but cutting notches while perched on a log six feet above the deck is terrifying.

I interrupt Nancy's progress peeling logs on a constant basis. I need another pair of hands every time I turn around. She cranks the skyhook's winch and helps me muscle the logs into place and put them into position on the wall. She drills holes to countersink the spikes and then pounds home the spikes with the sledge hammer. I could keep a crew of two or three young guys busy if I had them, if we could afford them. But it's just Nancy and I.

Each weekend we make a little more progress. It seems ridiculous to spend two days of hard work and only manage to get the walls one course higher all the way around. We Americans are used to building walls with dimension lumber in a matter of minutes, nailing a wall of 2x4s together on the floor and standing it up. But, Nancy and I are working like the tortoise not the rabbit, slow and steady, one log at a time.

We take pictures and show them to our workmates in Yellowstone. Some of our colleagues are fascinated and some are bored hearing about it over and over. One day our boss, Kathleen, a Montana native, tells me, " I must know five hundred people who say they want to build their own log cabin, but you guys are the only ones I know who are actually doing it." We find this to be amusing and true as well; we're the only ones we know building our own log cabin.

We quit work on the cabin at 4:45 every afternoon, generally exhausted. We trudge up the slope to our camp site, and just before we pass the outhouse, we turn around and take in the view. We gaze at our progress for a few minutes to absorb it all. What we see are the log walls with a few more logs on them, the door and window bucks sticking up into the air and the Absarokas off in the distance. It's a most beautiful sight.

Besides our weary arms and legs, we quit at 4:45 because NPR news comes on at 5:00 and there is 15 minutes of local news preceding it. We catch up on what's happening in Montana and the world. Down in Yellowstone we have no TV and no radio stations reach the South Entrance. We see a newspaper once a week if we're lucky. The Internet is now a reality for others, but we have only heard about it, we've never seen it or used it. So for two and a quarter hours every evening, we're glued to the radio. We hear about the deaths of former Supreme Court Justice Warren Burger, and entertainers Wolfman Jack and Jerry Garcia. Unfortunately, most nights we're treated to surreal updates on the progress of the O.J. Simpson trial.

We drink our cold beers, replenishing some of the fluids we've lost working in the hot sun. Nancy cooks dinner and I do the dishes. The little storage shed, the second building on our property, has now become the cook shed, our kitchen. Our dining room is around the campfire, which has major entertainment value. We sit in our Adirondack chairs each evening, drink our last glass of wine and plan tomorrow's activities, which really don't change that much. Eventually, and usually quite early, we head off to our bedroom, which is the tipi, and crawl into our sleeping bags.

Early July brings my family to Montana to see what all the fuss is about. They have rented a house on Trail Creek road between Bozeman and Livingston. Nancy and I take a couple of days off to entertain them, so we hike up Sacajawea Peak and raft the Yellowstone River with the gang. One day they all come up to the cabin site and peel logs, pound spikes and get some idea of what our living conditions are like. They are not overly impressed, really, and I'm not surprised. We only have a few log courses in place. It feels nothing at all like an enclosed structure. The pile of cut logs is more notable than the cabin itself. The skyhook's ability to move logs impresses them. And the kids like peeling the rapidly drying logs of their bark. They think the tipi is cool. But I'm not sure they can visualize the cabin as it appears so clearly in my mind.

By late July, we have four or five log courses in place. Come late September we are eight courses high and pleased as punch with our progress. We have about one month of work remaining down at the South Entrance. Fall is upon us and winter is coming soon. We're almost done building with logs, and another phase is about to begin. It's time to start thinking about the roof structure, the front and back porches and the staircase.

South side, snow on the ground, just before the roof rafters go up.

Doug

14

WORKING AGAINST THE CLOCK

*I talk to people who are musicians, and they go, Oh this is hell.
And I go, Are you kidding me? You never put tar paper on a roof,
did ya?*

-- Chris Isaak

About the time late October rolls around, we finish with

our jobs at the South Entrance, and we are also done building the log
walls. Our bank account is pretty flush because we have little to
spend it on. A monthly check from the folks who are renting our
house pays our modest mortgage with a little left over. Right now,

we don't have any land line phone bills, cable TV bills, gas utility bills, electricity bills, or garbage pickup fees. Our land payment is unremarkable. We were paying a small amount of rent to the Park Service for lodging, and we have some pretty regular gasoline bills, but gas is only $1.25 a gallon. Other than some food, beer and wine, we are spending very little. For a little longer, we have two paychecks coming in and not much going out. It's a great situation.

We have purchased some tools over the summer; among them a new Porter-Cable drill, a gasoline powered generator, and another chain saw, this time a little "disposable" $99 Homelite. We've been working all summer with the logs as our main building component, which of course, are free.

This is all about to change. We need to pay cash for all the roof materials; dimension lumber for the rafters and gable walls, the roof sheathing, insulation, nails and screws, roofing felt, metal roofing and other items too numerous to mention.

We've gambled that we will get winter-time job offers in some National Park Service unit that is, theoretically, down south where winter will pass us by. We've certainly sent out enough applications. We check our mailbox in Livingston as frequently as we can. But no one seems to want a couple of rangers in their late 40's with almost no Park Service experience.

Our new, first, cell phone is checked every day at noon for messages. We use it to keep in touch with our families and friends, price lumber and place our orders. When we run the generator to power the drill or an electric saw, we also charge up our bag phone. It's not a phone you can carry in your pocket; it's mainly a battery in a black faux leather bag the size of a loaf of bread with a phone attached. Nonetheless, it works great. September and October go by and we hear nothing from the Park Service. "Plan A" has not yet materialized and our "Plan B" has not yet been formulated. We don't know what we'll do if we don't get jobs, so we decide we'll worry about that when the snow flies.

A new load of lumber gets delivered by the six-wheel drive flatbed and tomorrow we'll be able to begin our work with dimension lumber. But first, we need to put up the beams that will support the loft floor. We pick out a very stout log and make a center post out of it. It sits on a device that is basically a big, oversize screw. Now remember, our logs will continue to shrink for a year or two. The support beams are going to sit on this center post like the arms on a "T". They will also rest on the walls themselves. When the log walls shrink, we need to let the center post down, little by little, to match the height of the walls. Therefore, every two months or so, for the next two years, I will get down on the floor and with a big crescent wrench, back the screw off a turn to drop it about a half inch. Sometimes I will hear some creaking and groaning, other times not a peep.

Initially, we keep the rocket launcher around for a few days thinking we might use it for something, but after a while we realize it's just in the way. We are forced to move it all around the deck not because we are using it, but because it's right where I want to set the ladder. I dismantle it and stack the lumber in the pile. Later on, before all the dimension lumber is covered with drywall, I often spot a rafter or a floor joist that I recognize as part of the old rocket launcher. Generally, I give that hunk of wood a loving pat as if to say "Good job, buddy."

The Montana weather continues with very typical and very beautiful fall days, one after the other. We get cloudless blue skies, dry and sunny. It warms up each day so that we can shed our jackets and gloves and work in T-shirts and it stays warm into the late afternoon. But the nightly campfires by the kitchen shed begin to feel better and better with each passing evening. We wear our sweatshirts and gloves a little longer each day. One morning as we're making our cowboy coffee, we find a layer of ice on O'Malley's water bucket and we know it's only a matter of time before winter chases us away from our cabin until spring.

The first beam is set in place with help from the Rocket Launcher.
The floor joists for the second story will sit on this beam.

But for now, we have no deadlines, no other place to be and no reason to track the days of the week. NPR lets us know it's the weekend when we hear the subtle change in programming on Saturday morning. On Sundays, we take a day off and we go down to Livingston. Nancy goes to the laundromat and washes our filthy laundry, goes food shopping and meanwhile, I watch the Denver Broncos in a local watering hole. Then our day off is over and we head back up the hill and get ready for Monday.

It is rather remarkable but we find, using a tape measure and our water/wine filled clear plastic tube, the corners of the log walls are within an inch of being the same height. All through the wall building process we have alternated logs so that we don't stack a butt end on a butt end, or a tip end on a tip end. It is remarkable because we are talking about logs that are randomly sized at the tip and butt ends. As I stacked the logs I would measure the distance off the floor at the completion of each course, and make adjustments on the successive courses, mainly by cutting a notch slightly deeper or shallower. And it has been successful. I wondered more than once if it was all going to work out in the end, and indeed it does.

The floor joists go up with lightning speed. We're shocked and astonished that the process goes so fast. We can lift these pieces of lumber without mechanical advantage, using just our arms and hands. They are light and dry, straight and planed and have a nice bull-nosed edged to cut down on splinters. Our tools are now a framing hammer instead of a three-pound sledge, 16 penny nails instead of 14 inch spikes, skilsaw rather than a chainsaw Working seven days a week with the dimension lumber seems to go so quickly mostly because our frame of reference is working with heavy, difficult to maneuver logs just two days out of the week. And we marvel at the old-timers, before modern dimension lumber made the components a standard size, and how good they must have been dealing with not-so-slight variations in all their building materials.

Our other tools are a long string, a string level and a four-foot level. The string, when stretched across the top of the joist, tells me when the floor supports are in the same plane, or flat. The string level is a tiny device that rides on a taut string and gives an approximation of horizontal. The four-foot level tells me plumb across one joist from wall to beam, and from joist to joist. To make a flat floor I either manipulate the uneven surface of the log or the joist itself with the saw or hatchet, but in the end they are pretty darn plumb.

Next we put down a deck of plywood where the loft will be and begin thinking about putting up rafters. We are working alone, just the two of us. I am head carpenter, Nancy is my "gofer" and extra set of hands. I have to think of ways to accomplish a whole host of difficult tasks with just ourselves as labor. For the most part it goes pretty well. Nancy is a trooper, working hard, lifting more than her share and generally tolerant of my mistakes and rantings.

The first task toward putting up the roof framing is to raise a ridge-beam, a long 2x10, temporarily held up in the air by some 2x4s. We add some more 2x4 braces to keep it in place and mark off the positions of the rafters. I have put together a rough drawing of my roof plan. It contains two shed dormers on the south facing side, because that's where the view is, and also where the winter sun is. Were I to do it all over again, I'd add dormers on the north side to add both light and ventilation, but windows are not cheap, and hindsight is not foresight. And, make no mistake, I am already plenty challenged with the framing of the two dormers as it is.

We make steady progress and each day as we walk up the hill to our camp, we still look back and assess our progress. The rafters begin to define the roofline, and the roof framing begins to establish a very handsome shape to the cabin. Accustomed to looking at the walls only, the roof has been just something we've had to imagine. Viewing the log walls without the roof structure makes them appear squat and heavy, but as soon as we have enough rafters in place, the whole cabin begins to look lighter and, very curiously, more substantial at the same time. The experience I acquired several months before building the outhouse and the shed roofs, now comes in very handy. In fact, this is not the first peaked, gable roof I've ever built, just the largest.

Cutting one of the last notches on one of the last logs. The skyhook can be seen in the upper left.

The north side of the roof covers the north side porch and it appears, suddenly, very cozy, protected and sheltered. It looks like it will be a great place to hang some tools out of the weather, like the splitting maul and the ax. And it seems like the north side porch will be a nice place to sit on a hot summer day, gazing out into the forest where I know I will eventually see grazing deer and browsing elk and moose. It's only a matter of time.

But this morning we wake up, open the door of our tipi and find we have a few inches of snow. Time is running out on this building season, but we are prepared to stick with it as long as we can, at least until the weather drives us out. We still have no plan for the coming winter, but we talk about places to visit farther south. A list begins to form in our minds of friends we know who wouldn't mind a couple of visitors for a few days. We call our friends from the South Entrance, Joe and Linda, the retirees from Maryville, Tennessee, to inquire if they still want a couple of house sitters for the month of January. They do, and so, a plan begins to form in our minds. We have friends or relatives in Bozeman, Denver, the little village of Cuba, New Mexico, and the metropolises of Mesa, Arizona, Houston, Texas, and the Calumet Region of Indiana; and we can housesit for a month in the green hills of Tennessee. Later on we might head out to Vashon Island, Washington for a visit with my sister. We think about some backpacking trips we can take in the cold, but snowless canyons of southern Utah.

We are determined to get the roof sheathing on before the snow really begins to pile up. But first, we must build some knee walls to help support the roof rafters and define the spaces up in the loft. There are also two dormers to frame up, not to mention framing the back porch, the front porch and the porch roof on the south side. There is much to do and we work at least eight hours a day, six days a week. Still, it seems like things are going well and at a pretty good clip.

While Nancy and I suffer and work our fingers to the bone, O'Malley is in doggie Shangri-la. He sleeps with us in the tipi but has no problem going out the tipi door and howling at the moon or taking a leak. He sleeps on a rug on the frigid ground, with his tail curled up over his nose on the coldest nights. The big lug goes to the worksite with us every day and hangs out in a sunny place, or under the floor deck, depending on the weather. Watching the campfire with us in the evening seems very enjoyable for him. At times we have to jump up and brush sparks off his coat when we smell the singed hair. He never feels the spark and seems to think we are playing a wonderful game. With much bravado, he keeps squirrels and chipmunks and magpies away from the worksite, the campfire, the cook shed and the tipi. He likes to run ahead of or alongside the pickup on the way down to the county road and back up the hill when we return. O'Malley really couldn't be any happier. And although we're working as hard as we ever have in our lives, with very few comforts of home and only a radio and book for entertainment and diversion, we're just as happy as O'Malley.

We are going through money fairly quickly now, buying plywood, OSB, and 2x4s. The lumber company will no longer deliver the items to the house site with the snow on the ground. But it is only a minor distraction. I have them dump everything at the bottom of the hill and haul it up in old Rusty who now wears two sets of chains. I find it very enjoyable to drive the pickup with chains on all fours. It handles like a tank and seems to be able to crawl up any hill through quite a bit of snow. It's very impressive where this old Ford will go in 4WD, low range, chains all-around, and a load of lumber in the bed. It busts through ice covered puddles, crawls down icy, frozen, rutted two-track roads and plows through snow up to the axle. But I know a few more inches of snow will screw up the whole deal. Enough snow and any truck will be defeated. I begin to wonder about buying a snowmobile, which until now has been a very dirty word.

I've heard that boaters very quickly place themselves into two separate groups; the sail boater or the power boater, and the two are not known to mingle very well or very often. Up to this point I've been a skier who had nothing but scorn for the idiots who drive snowmobiles, also known as "Bubbleheads' due to their helmets. Hikers have no love for dirt bikers or ATV riders, and vice-versa and seldom does anyone practice both disciplines. I absolutely hate recreational jeepers, off-roaders and those who spend more money on a rock-crawler than they do on their child's education. They're like mobile environmental disasters. My philosophy is simple: These motorized conveyances are tools, not toys and those who use them for recreation are fools. But here I am enjoying blasting through the snow in my 4WD, meanwhile I'm considering buying a snowmobile. The irony is thick enough to cut with an ax.

I give Nancy a job I haven't yet found time enough to do myself. I draw a diagram and we measure and set some stakes. I ask her to dig the holes for the south-facing, front porch footers. The footers will sit very close to the edge of the rock face, and the porch will cantilever over the rocks so that you can stand on the edge of the porch and look almost straight down. Nancy scrapes away the snow and starts digging holes until she reaches bedrock, which in this case is actually less than a foot. When she's all done, we pour footers, not caring what elevation they are. Redwood 4x4s will sit on the piers and support the weight of the porch. While the rafters are too slippery with frost in the morning to climb upon, we work in the warm sunlight and frame out the front porch.

Sheathing the roof takes at least a week. It's possible to reach many places with a ladder, or from the loft floor, but eventually I have to crawl between the rafters and get up on the roof to nail down the sheathing. I haven't done this since working in Crested Butte for Bill's construction company, back when I was 23, flexible, lithe, athletic and fearless. Now, I'm a very tentative 47, carrying too much weight and not particularly agile. Of all the tasks I've undertaken since starting to build our cabin, this is the most taxing. After a short stint on the roof, fear makes me overly cautious, and the 9/12 pitch makes my ankles and legs scream with agony. I find that the soles of the insulated rubber and leather boots I'm wearing grip the OSB as well as can be expected, as long as the surface is dry. If I hit a shady spot it could be a short trip to the ground. Working near the center of the roof, and near the peak is not particularly a problem, but approaching the edge, any edge, is terrifying. I conclude that being a roofer is probably the world's worst job.

I run into a few problems. If you will recall, the piers turned out to form something less than a perfect rectangle. I am now paying the price for those early errors because the roof is, quite naturally, a little out of square as well. It's nothing that can't be dealt with, after all, OSB roof sheathing is very easy to cut. There is no way in hell that I'm going to be able to or want to put the metal roof on this place. So I know the roofer will have some geometry problems to solve. It's nothing that will be noticed with the naked eye, but a tape measure will detect it.

Once the roof sheathing is on we come to a standstill. We find nothing more that we can do until spring. There is no question that it's too cold to work without gloves, and too difficult to accomplish anything with them on. It's becoming hard to get materials up to the site, as well as food and water. It takes longer every day to deal with frozen water buckets and ice-cold hands and feet. Obviously, it's time to leave for the winter.

The tipi is frozen in place and it's no longer possible to take it down. It will certainly be standing when we return, but what shape will the canvas be in? We stash our sleeping bags, tools, chainsaws and everything that can be carried away into the cook shed and put a padlock on it. We've put all remaining food into airtight, and hopefully, mouse-proof containers. Everything we can think of to make our eventual return problem free, we've already done. We stuff our backpacks as full as possible with clothes and gear we can't leave behind, pull them on, and Nancy, O'Malley and I trudge through the snow to where we've left Rusty.

Doug

15

NOMADIC WINTER

If you don't know where you are going, any road will get you there.
– Lewis Carroll

We drive Rusty down the hill to where our used Ford Escort station wagon sits at the end of the county road and the end of 2WD terrain. We spend a little while removing the chains from the pickup. Nancy jumps in the Escort, which we have failed to name since it has so little personality, and we head down the hill to I-90 in both vehicles. We are leaving old Rusty with friends for the winter while we travel in the Escort.

Our first stop is just over the hill in Bozeman. We spend several weeks staying at the house of Nancy's former boss while they are visiting their grown kids. It is rather luxurious for us to have all the modern conveniences that we've been without since renting out our house and splitting time between our housing in Yellowstone and the tipi. Not only do we have a land-line phone where most calls are free, we have a kitchen sink and a dishwasher. We have access to cable TV and a VCR which we use quite a bit since we haven't watched a movie since early May. The house is heated, of course, and we sleep in beds with clean sheets. We have a washer and dryer to use any time we want, so our clothes no longer smell like sweat and smoke. We are truly relishing the things most Americans take for granted on a daily basis.

For us, all those luxuries pale in comparison to the bathroom with toilet and shower. I probably take as many showers in two weeks as I took the entire summer. Someone said a civilization is judged by how we treat the least among us, but historians and archeologists judge a civilization, in part, by the quality of its plumbing. In any case we are being treated well and have plenty of quality plumbing, for the time being.

We seek out old Bozeman friends we haven't seen much of lately. Some still seem to think we are a little crazy, and others are envious of our total freedom. A couple of weeks go by in a flash. Now we hit the road for real. Denver is our next stop where I have family and we have a few old friends from our Colorado days. We spend a few days with my middle sister and family and a night with old friends we used to work with. We stop for a few days with friends John and Eileen, Nancy's old tipi buddy. They are living in Montrose, Colorado and John and Eileen are intrigued with our cabin adventure. John is tantalized with pictures of the construction of the cabin while Eileen is excited, naturally, by pictures of the tipi.

Good fortune graces us; while we are in a bookstore in downtown Montrose, we find a self-published book about collecting water from rooftops. It's really an answer to our dreams. It is a highly illustrated, hand written book that gives us a rough blueprint for collecting water off the roof of our cabin. We don't have to re-invent the wheel after all, someone has already done it. The next day we say goodbye to John and Eileen and it's off to southern Utah for a backpacking trip.

Fish and Owl Creek Canyons are a gorgeous hike and we re-discover that a backpacking tent is quite cramped and downright uncomfortable compared to a tipi. It's warm and sunny during the short day but downright cold during the long night. We wish we had a barrel stove to warm up our frozen and tired bodies, but all we have is a campstove and a tiny (and illegal) campfire to warm us. We've packed in plenty of warm clothes, but we're still chilled to the bone from our long walk. The stars seem to be especially bright in this cold and clear desert air.

From southern Utah, we head for the strange little town of Cuba, New Mexico. It sits on the edge of the Navajo Reservation and is mostly populated with a mixture of Native Americans and Mexican-Americans. Our friends Suzi and Bob are teachers on the reservation and old friends of Nancy's from her days at Western State College in Gunnison. They treat us to a visit to Chaco Culture National Historical Park. It's a long haul over some bad roads, but there is clearly evidence that at one time there was a high degree of civilization in the Four Corners Region. Back in Cuba, we catch up with our collective histories. We haven't seen much of Suzi and Bob since they moved away from Bozeman and there is a lot to discuss. We could probably stay with Suzi and Bob all winter, drinking beer and wine, talking and laughing long into the night and sleeping in our sleeping bags on their living room floor and they wouldn't complain, but we have other places to visit during our long nomadic winter.

The next stop is with Nancy's high school friend Marianne and her husband, Gary, in Mesa, Arizona. Nancy and Marianne spend a day over at a friend's house making the traditional Feliz Navidad season tamales. They work all day doing whatever it takes to make them, cooking and shredding the pork, making the tamale dough and wrapping them in corn husks. Meanwhile Gary, O'Malley and I go on a desert hike up Weaver's Needle in the Superstition Mountains, a rock formation which is composed of volcanic tuff eroded into a spire that imitates the Saguaro growing all around it. The winter weather these few weeks before Christmas is like a summer day in Yellowstone. Crackling dry air, cloudless sky, bright sunshine and temperatures in the mid-60s. We all arrive back at their house around the same time. In the back yard, Gary and I suck down beers and O'Malley slurps water, trying to replace all the moisture we've lost over the day. Then we sit down to a fabulous meal of, what else, home-made tamales. Like Suzi and Bob, Marianne and Gary's hospitality is boundless and they let us know that we homeless waifs can stay as long as we want. But we're now on a tight schedule until the last day of January. We stay two or three nights and prepare to move on.

We pack up the Ford Escort and head east on I-10, destination Houston, Texas. The big pueblo on the Buffalo Bayou, H-Town, Magnolia City, the capital of the Sunbelt. My little sister lives in Houston, not a half mile from the Buffalo Bayou and we are going to spend Christmas with her. She's recently split up with her husband and has a list of home repair tasks for Nancy and me to tackle while we are here. We buy some Christmas gifts, walk O'Malley and Amy's dogs in the park, visit the house sided with beer cans, take in the Mark Rothko museum, antique shops, and have great dinners at various ethnic restaurants.

Nancy, Amy and I drink beer at nearby Jimmy's Ice House. Houston has a bunch of these ice houses, which are a relic of the days before air conditioning. What they remind me of is a re-purposed gas station with their large overhead garage doors. They are a little bit town hall, part tavern, and have been a South Texas tradition since the 1920s. Icehouses stored and distributed block ice for the neighborhood iceboxes. As times changed they diversified selling cold beer, a little food, offering a cool, air-conditioned spot where neighbors and families come to sit, talk, play some checkers, and listen to music.

We didn't anticipate we would like Houston, but we find it to be a vibrant and lively city full of fun. No ethnic minority seems to be lacking. The city is diverse; black, white, Asian and Mexican and cultural mixtures like Cajun and Creole. The downside is the horrendous traffic, the foul air and constant noise, but we're very environmentally sensitive given our recent life of near wilderness-like quiet and solitude. Nancy and I find it very strange to sit outside on the back porch, on what we mountain dwellers consider a balmy evening, and see the glow of city lights reflecting off the cloudy sky. No stars visible whatsoever and we hear the continuous rumble of traffic on Interstates 10, 610 and 45.

The last day of 1995, we pack the car with O'Malley and everything else we have brought with us, backpacking and camping gear strapped to the roof, bound for Maryville, Tennessee. Arkansas is beautiful and rural, full of hills, trees and fallow farm fields. We spend the night in a motel somewhere near Memphis on the western side of the Mississippi River. Since we left our tipi back in November, this is about the third night in a motel. I can remember motel stays, once in Colorado and once in Texas. We haven't busted the bank yet and our credit card bills are manageable.

The next day, January 1, we arrive in Maryville. Joe and Linda welcome us to their lovely house in a very beautiful part of Tennessee. They are leaving for Florida in two days in their big motor home, the same one they spend their summers in at the South Entrance of Yellowstone. Joe and Linda escort us around the area the next day, showing us downtown Maryville, the grocery stores,

liquor stores, making sure we can find our way around when they leave.

Maryville is the Tennessee gateway to Great Smokies National Park and Cades Cove. Also nearby are the Appalachian Trail, Dolly Parton's Pigeon Forge amusement park and the gorgeous Smoky Mountains studded with log cabins, old and new and every age in between. Cades Cove, settled just after the War of 1812 is a peaceful, grassy valley situated within the National Park. It is a historical gold mine of post-revolution American culture. Due to its isolation much of it is very well preserved. We are interested, mainly, in the numerous log cabins in the Cove and it turns out they are invariably gorgeous. The Park Service has done an excellent job of restoring them and keeping the area, if not totally historically accurate, superbly beautiful.

Our Montana cabin will be without electricity, a source of water and other modern conveniences, and Cades Cove and the theme park provides us with many clues as to how we will conduct our lives without them. The Forest Service and Park Service cabins are still a great model, but we find these Appalachian cabins fascinating. As we comb through the Cades Cove cabins, such as the John Oliver cabin built in 1822, we are enthralled with every feature and construction detail. Others don't pay nearly so much attention. As we crawl though every space in every cabin, we see visitors who barely spend two minutes in a cabin, no longer than it takes to walk in and walk out. It's like trying to see all of Yellowstone in an afternoon.

Not only do we see Cades Cove, but we visit an early American life theme park, a couple of log cabins for sale with a real estate agent, log home demonstration homes, and literally anything with "log" or "cabin" in the name. We were clueless when we agreed to be house sitters here in Maryville, but it turns out to be a very informative and instructional time period.

We learn to truly love this part of Tennessee. We spend almost every day exploring the area and put lots of miles on the Ford Escort. We hike the Appalachian Trail for a few miles and discover that not everything "Back East" is inferior to the West. The trail is unbelievably magnificent, and we are surprised that, unlike the Rockies, you gain elevation, lose it, regain it, lose it again, and so on and so forth until you are exhausted, no matter the lower elevation. The fallen leaves litter the trail so heavily that we can't see it very well. O'Malley knows where it is though and runs like a deer along the trail, chasing the scent of critters that he can't see.

Our explorations take us to eastern Tennessee - Knoxville, Johnson City, Gatlinburg, and Dayton, the site of the famous "Monkey Trial". We visit the highest point in the East, Mount Mitchell in North Carolina, at 6,684 feet it's about the same elevation as our cabin. All in all, we enjoy our time in Tennessee.

The last day of January, Joe and Linda come home and the next morning we head up through Kentucky to Berlin, Ohio, where the Lehman Brothers have a store. We've seen their catalog. It is a hardware store that supplies the Amish with non-electrical appliances with respect to their religious beliefs, and it boasts an impressive number of items that apply to our needs in our off-the-grid cabin. We spend a couple of hours poking around the store and come away with a few items that we decide we can't live without. Our most expensive purchase is an Aladdin lamp, fueled by pressurized lamp oil, and equipped with a mantle like a Coleman lantern. It quietly casts a light that outshines any kerosene lamp we've ever seen.

On our way back to Montana, we stop over in Indiana to visit all of Nancy's relatives in the Calumet Region. It's my first visit to Indiana and I am meeting Nancy's brother, Jim, and his family for the first time. We spend most of our time with Nancy's mom and dad at their new address in a retirement home. Nancy's mom is suffering from Alzheimer's and is in the adjacent nursing home. Ed religiously makes twice daily visits to Sue. Nancy is shocked to see her mother's recent deterioration and prefers to remember her as the woman whom she describes a little "Steamroller". I remember that woman too and find it hard to reconcile her with this end-of-life patient who has been stripped of all dignity and humanity. We have no way of knowing, but this is Nancy's last opportunity to visit with her father. Less than a year later he will be gone.

We proudly show our photos of the cabin-in-progress to Nancy's dad and the rest of the family, but like many others on this journey, they have no frame of reference for our strange behavior. It is as if we are speaking some foreign language and they cannot understand what we are doing and more significantly, why on earth we would want to do it? We're disappointed but not surprised. I suppose it's like stamp collecting or sky-diving, you either understand someone's passion or you don't. In any case, Jim, Ed and the rest of the family, Nancy too, are rightly preoccupied with Sue's precarious health and we understand. We tell ourselves that someday the family will visit our cabin and understand, but it never comes to pass.

Nancy wants to see her old neighborhood so we make a drive by her childhood home. She's surprised to see how tiny it seems. We visit Nancy's Aunt Helen where 120 pound O'Malley romps in the back yard with 15 pound Spikey like they have always been the best of friends. The extended family gathers for meals and recollections and is excited to see Nancy, who has left the Region for good. It's a bittersweet time for us, being around this tightly knit family and all the old memories.

After a few days of family dinners and family stories we're a little homesick, ready to go home. But in all reality, we have no home to go to. We're in a quandary. Should we rent a house for a few months? Spend our savings that we'll soon need to buy building material? Throw our renters out of our house? We're not absolutely certain we have our jobs in the Park come May, but we've been verbally promised positions.

We spend the night on the road in Belle Fourche, South Dakota, and call our friends Karen and Okey in Bozeman to see if we can spend a night or two with them. They reply that they have been thinking about us and have a deal we can't refuse. Come on, they say.

In Bozeman, Okey explains that their summer house on Lake Qu'Appelle in Saskatchewan needs some work. If we want to go up there we can stay for as long as a month. Qu'Appelle, in my high-school French, means "What Name." It's situated out in the prairie near the town of Fort Qu'Appelle, not far from an Indian

Reservation. I call my sister on Vashon Island, Washington, and she has a deal for us as well. They want a small garage on their property converted to something resembling an extra bedroom. These deals sound like they might get us into May. So we agree to go both places, Fort Qu'Appelle and Vashon, but first we spend a week buying a snowmobile and a sled and spend a few nights in our tipi.

It's something which we know absolutely nothing about - snowmobiles, but we look at a few used ones. I've driven one once. We agree to buy an old Arctic Cat from a dealer and we buy a cargo sled to pull behind it. The dealer gives me some lessons in the snow-covered back lot, a host of tips and sound advice. Some work is involved to get the snow machine into the back of Rusty, but a pile of snow in the parking lot makes a fine ramp. A visit to the grocery store and we're off to see what we can accomplish up at our fledgling cabin.

It's mid-February but the snow hasn't piled up too deep, thankfully. I'm able to blaze a trail into the cabin through the virgin snow. A few inches deeper and I probably would not have made it. The advice from the snowmobile dealer comes in handy. He's told me to widen the trail by one ski width each time I pass, until I make a solid trail. I make several trips up and down the hill, learning that the tipi and the cabin are still standing. Meanwhile, Nancy loads the sled with our gear. We hook up the trailer/sled and get a running start up the hill. O'Malley runs along behind us, thinking no doubt, that this is a great game.

We huddle in our frozen tipi while I get a fire going in the barrel stove. In no time at all the tipi is as warm as a tropical beach and we are stripping off our heavy coats, gloves and hats. We have brought with us two more sleeping bags, meaning we now have a total of five. The plan is to use our synthetic fill, summer weight bags that we bought for our European bicycle trip inside of our down bags. We'll have the fifth sleeping bag unzipped so it's flat and thrown over us like a comforter. Wood burns quickly in the barrel stove and I realize I'm going to have to spend some time tomorrow to find some dead trees nearby and turn them into firewood.

The cook shed still has some dried food, dishes, utensils, our cook top and propane bottle so making a meal takes little time. The cookstove and the propane lantern are enough to begin to warm up the little shed even though it's totally un-insulated. We never imagined we'd find ourselves actually using it as a kitchen but it's doing a passable job. We find our hands and head are perfectly warm but our legs are cold and our feet are absolutely freezing on the plywood floor.

In the time it takes us to cook and eat dinner the small hot fire goes out and the tipi interior returns to the same temperature as outside. As soon as we turn out the lantern and crawl into our five sleeping bags the quiet envelops us. There is an almost complete silence, broken only by the breathing of O'Malley on several rugs, and the crackle of the fire in the stove. When the fire goes out the stove begins to make small, almost imperceptible popping sounds of contracting metal. Pretty soon it is silent and beginning to get cold. I worry about poor O'Malley, but he doesn't seem uncomfortable under his heavy black coat. I get up several times during the night to start a fire. When I step out of the tipi to take a leak, it is only marginally warmer inside. There is no thermal mass to hold the heat and no insulation to keep it from passing through the canvas almost immediately.

Morning comes and while we're sipping our hot coffee and listening to the radio in the cook shed we're surprised, no, astonished is a better word, to learn that it is 28 below zero in Bozeman. It could be a few degrees warmer or colder where we're huddled, but it's damn cold any way you look at it.

We stay about a week, not getting much work done. A load of lumber gets hauled up the hill in the snowmobile and trailer and I am able to deck the north side porch which is under the roof. But it's almost impossible to work in the cold. It never warms up enough to stop thinking how damn cold it is. We spend most of our time melting ice, cutting firewood, heating water and feeding the fire in the stove. We imagine that someday we'll be toasty warm around the big woodstove in our comfy cabin and laugh at our frozen week in the tipi. We make a decision: it can't be too much colder in

Saskatchewan. We pack up our gear and a bunch of tools and ride the snow machine down to the bottom of the hill, cover it with a tarp, load the Ford Escort and point it toward Canada.

The task Okey has given us is to install a hot water heater and construct a shower in their summer home. After we acquaint ourselves with the town of Fort Qu'Appelle, find a grocery store, video store, liquor store and hardware store we begin to settle in to the cottage. It's comfortable, not luxurious, but we're happy. It has electric heat and a nice little fireplace and a huge stack of wood. The cabin is on the lake and draws its water supply from deep below the ice. The lines are drained for the winter so we fill bottles of water from the neighbor's house or in town. The toilet situation, since there is no running water, I will leave to your imagination. Mainly it involves a substantial supply of plastic bags. For entertainment, we have a TV which gets no reception although it works with the VCR, and on the radio the marvelous Canadian Broadcasting Corporation, so we're happy. It could be worse.

Nothing stands in our way of constructing the shower stall. Not even the metric system. We connect plumbing, buy a small electric hot water heater, run some wires, install some switches, and do everything but try it out. There's no water so there is not a thing we can do except hope that when Okey and Karen come up to Fort Qu'Appelle in August, the whole contraption will work. Meanwhile, we're forced to heat water on the stove and take take sponge baths. For a real luxurious shower experience, we drive down the road to a campground that's open all winter.

Nancy, O'Malley and I take long walks on the frozen lake. At first we're tentative about walking on the ice. Will it hold us? But once we see cars and trucks and snowmobiles driving on the ice we're pretty convinced it's nice and thick. We look into an abandoned fishing hole and discover the ice is at least a foot thick, oops, make that 30.4 centimeters, or maybe more. It is eerie, however, to be standing on the ice when it shifts and loudly cracks. Fear strikes at my bowels and I imagine disappearing under the ice and suffering an agonizing death.

Nancy used the time while we were in Bozeman to apply for an Interpretive Ranger position in Yellowstone. One day she makes a phone call from our little cottage in Saskatchewan and finds she has a job in Grant Village starting in late May. I'm told my job at the South Entrance is open, but I beg off making a decision for as long as possible.

Boredom begins to take its toll after about three weeks. We think of heading out to Washington State. It's mid-March and spring can't be far away out there in Puget Sound. Again we pack the trusty Escort and head south to the States. We head across the Montana high-line from Plentywood on to Wolf Point, Glasgow, Malta, Harlem and Havre for the night. We pass through Chester, Shelby and Cut Bank and finally stop in Browning and call some old friends we haven't seen in years. They've found a lovely old ranch house to rent, tucked up against the side of a mountain and the Forest Service boundary. Eric comes to meet us in Browning and plows his 4WD Ford, a carbon copy of Rusty except for color, through the snow to the house where we are greeted by Colleen and the dogs.

Eric is intrigued by our pictures of the cabin construction like no one else we've encountered on this journey. He examines each photo in detail and has a number of insightful questions about every facet of the job. I can see that he imagines himself doing this same thing when the time is right for him and Colleen. Late into the night, we talk over old times in Denver, eat too much spaghetti and drink way too much red wine. Finally, our fatigue overtakes us; we throw our sleeping bags on their spare bed and sleep like the dead.

In the morning, Colleen makes us coffee and breakfast while we nurse our sore heads with aspirin and fluids. Off to Vashon Island we go, hoping to make good time over the Rockies and down to I-90, out of Montana, across the panhandle of Idaho, and beyond the Columbia onto the fertile stretches of eastern Washington. Then over the snowy Cascades and down the big hill into Seattle, and every mile the air grows more humid, the landscape more green and the formerly icy roads are suddenly covered with water.

Vashon Island is just a ferry ride from West Seattle. But it's a rough enough journey that Vashon is more of a stand-alone village than a bedroom community for Seattle. No mistake, the ferries are full every morning and evening, but more folks stay and work on the island than commute. It's very rural, with only one or two little conglomerations that could be called a town. My oldest sister and her husband have a couple of acres with a comfy house, a vegetable garden, some chickens and a lot of green grass. It's pretty well fenced, but not so well fenced that we don't have to go search for O'Malley every once in awhile. O'Malley is a very good dog while we visit my sister. He only kills one chicken and gets into a single fight with Willie, the Wheaten Terrier.

The main problem with my sister's house is the bedroom that we are sleeping in. It's called the "Cubby" because it is a bed with walls around it, like a big cupboard. One side is open with curtains hanging down for privacy. The ladies complain about how hard it is to change the sheets on this particular bed. The cubby is situated in a room that has the stairway and doors to the master bedroom and a tiny second bedroom. Darrell and Leslie want more guest space and think that the old one-car garage can be converted to a decent sized bedroom.

After breakfast we walk outside and look at the garage. Perhaps in the dry, arid west the building would have been worth saving, but we're in the Pacific Northwest and the building is only suitable for tearing down. The wood is rotted beyond being structurally sound. We can push a knife, or a screwdriver a half inch into the wood with very little effort.

We tear it down and start building a new structure called the "Rose Cottage". When done, it is very handsome. It's 12 x 16 feet with a loft in the rafters. A rope and pulley raise and lower a hinged stairway and keep it out of the way. A friend of Darrell's wires it for electricity and hooks it up to the house. It gets a bright red metal roof and we side it with cedar shingles. Darrell's a newspaper consultant and works from home, so every afternoon he can, he's outside in his work clothes tacking up shingles. We use salvage doors and windows, and when it's furnished with garage sale furniture and an electric heater, it's the cutest, coziest little bedroom I've ever seen.

It surprises us to learn that Darrell's electrician lives in a house that collects water from the roof. Not drinking water, but water to wash and flush the toilet. We quiz him for every detail of his system and he draws us a schematic of the collection, storage and filtering operations. Of course we won't have the endless supply of rain, but nonetheless, we are encouraged to learn someone is doing it.

It's a most wonderful four or five weeks. We enjoy spending time with Leslie and Darrell and they take good care of their indentured servants, feeding us well and keeping us entertained.

We stay until mid-May. Nancy's new job is about to start. We've decided that it makes most sense for me to work exclusively on the cabin this summer and perhaps it will be habitable by the time winter rolls around again. We pack the Escort for the final leg of our nomadic winter and head for the ferry terminal, bound for Montana.

Nancy

16

A BUCKET OF GOO

I haven't failed. I've found 10,000 ways that don't work.
-- Thomas Alva Edison

Doug approaches construction projects with near

scientific precision. He's very visually-oriented, and rarely starts a project without a raft of drawings in hand. Standard graph paper and mechanical pencil are his weapons of choice, but I've seen him equally fluid with a knife-whittled carpenter pencil on a hunk of 2x4. Page after page of elevations, side view, rear view, cross section, all leading to a visualization of the finished product in his mind. Little arrows shoot away from each drawing, expanding on particular aspects. Dimensions are recorded in a clear, orderly fashion. Along the way, drawings get tweaked, often significantly, or new drawings emerge.

When we have worked on renovation projects together, and I suggest an idea, Doug's automatic response is, "Draw me a picture." For me, this is akin to saying, "Shoot yourself in the foot." It is painful. And it rarely produces the desired result. I have little talent with pen and paper. So, when I am requested to transfer something that I can clearly see in my mind onto something more tangible, I feel approaching failure. My solution is to conserve the number of pencil strokes, and make my drawing as concise as possible. Doug would not use concise as the appropriate adjective. Perhaps drawing on a pinhead would be more accurate. I admire Doug's uncanny ability to sketch without ruler. The true testament of his skill, of course, is witnessing instant cognition on even a neophyte's face upon being shown one of the drawings. He sees that classic puzzled look and knows words alone will never do the trick.

Good drawings are necessary for good planning and good execution. They require patience and skill. I never have any worry about Doug's skill level. What he doesn't already know, he will learn. There are some projects and tasks, however, which he never develops a fondness for. He loves framing carpentry, where progress is immediate. Finish carpentry, those nagging final chores are always the hardest: that last piece of baseboard that has several odd cuts, or the tile to carpet threshold with a ½ inch height change. We tend to put these off, sometimes to the point where we no longer even notice them. They eventually get done, but require a type of patience that tends to escape him.

There is an area where Doug draws the line and will not cross. Mostly it involves, as we have come to describe it, the plastic arts. This category roughly includes things that come in a bucket or tube; caulk, thinset, grout, drywall mud, even paint. I don't know much about the chemical composition of these components, but there is a great deal of difference between how you work with lumber and how you work with drywall mud. The former can be measured, cut, sanded, drilled, hammered, literally beaten to a pulp, and then even re-used. Conversely, for example, drywall mud is a one-shot deal. Malleable in its initial form, it gets slapped on the wall, stroked into shape and left to dry. Its purpose is not for structure or insulation, but aesthetics.

Caulking, grouting, mudding, painting, these are the touches that, when done well, more-or-less go unnoticed. When done poorly, they are glaring eyesores. No way am I trying to say that I'm a pro at any of this, ever was or ever will be. I have certainly had more than a few moments of subversive pleasure, slinging plastic shit at the closest vertical surface, and calmly walking away. Working the plastic arts, and especially being able to do so without shame, requires lots of skill and substantially more patience.

In our building and renovation projects, the plastic arts fall to me by default. Who in their right mind would attempt to perfect such unglamorous tasks as running a smooth bead of caulk, cutting a crisp ceiling paint edge, mixing powder pigments to achieve a perfect tint, channel a well-rounded grout line, or achieve a flawless drywall texture? Since I have been assigned and resigned myself to these jobs, I am determined to learn to like it. In the end, I must admit I find it therapeutic; no, not some nirvana trance-like state, but definitely a lost in thought escape. Of course, books-on-tape help.

During the building phase of the cabin, I have always been Doug's helper. We work side by side, day after day. He is the mastermind, I the assistant. I just naturally assume that we will attack the chinking of the cabin in that partnership fashion. I guess I shouldn't be surprised when Doug suggests that I take on that project alone. It is one of the plastic arts, he reminds me.

In the style of log cabin building we are using, courses of logs are laid row upon row, overlapping at corners, and there are gaps between rows. Notches are carved out of each subsequent log laid down, which reduces the size of the gap. But a horizontal space along the length of the logs remains. These spaces must be covered on both the interior and exterior, with a dead air space created between, and then a protective coating applied. The logs will continue to shrink for a period of time, and definitely not at a consistent rate from log to log, so if the insulation or coating material is inflexible it presents problems.

In the United States, long before some of the areas were officially 'states', pioneers were building log cabins. The standard method of filling the spaces between the logs was chinking and daubing. Masters of using materials at hand, the builders first stuffed them with moss, clay, mud and straw or animal dung, no doubt depending upon what was in greatest supply. The cover coat, daubing, was a troweled finish layer of either lime or clay with various binder additives: horse hair, straw, sawdust, ashes or even newspaper.

Old pioneer cabins and original CCC-built National Forest Service cabins are elegant, graceful and many are still standing. The weathered logs, welcoming front porches with vast overhangs, mullioned windows, and human scale exhibit an architectural quality and design that has become lost in big box houses. Beautiful as they are, the old log cabins suffered with time. Chinking, often concrete, cracked and fell out, allowing moisture, wind and mice to lay siege to numerous back-country structures. Many have been rescued by modern-day chinking products. With clever brand names like Perma-Chink or Log-Jam, the tinted textured flexible acrylic goo contains no horse hair, animal dung, straw, or moss, at least as far as I know. But it sticks like glue, not only to logs, but to clothing, skin, ladders, and Sony Walkmans.

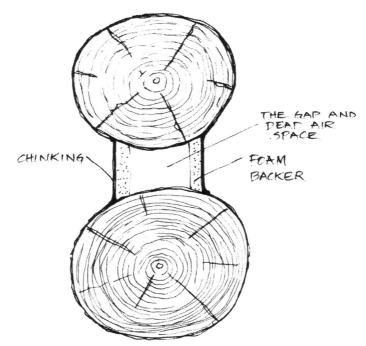

I approach my chinking assignment with trepidation. I am clueless as to correct tools, method of application, amount needed, even the right questions to ask. Doug suggests I get a small quantity to begin with, for a test run. That sounds good. I feel a little out of my league walking into Simpkins-Hallin in Bozeman the first time, and telling the guy behind the counter I was starting to chink our log cabin. Waiting behind me are some serious customers, commercial log-home builders, who are buying buckets of chink by the truck load. Slightly intimidated, I turn around and go exploring the aisles. A cross-section display illustrates the thickness of a very evenly applied application of chinking over a closed cell foam backer rod. The texture of the chink is like coarse sand, rough but pleasant to the touch. Even when it is 'cured' it remains flexible or slightly spongy. The backer rod foam replaces the pioneer filler of moss or mud. It is sold, as the name implies, in rod-like lengths or rolls in varying diameters to correspond to the gap in the logs. When I start calculating the cost of the backer rods times the number of gaps on our cabin, the multiplying dollar signs make me dizzy.

I spend way too long at the building materials store that afternoon, pondering my decisions. I keep forgetting this is only a test. Eventually I settle on a five gallon (53 lb) bucket of a light grey chink and a couple backer rods. Already the bill is over $100.00. For application tools, I opt to keep it real simple. Think cake decorating and the little frosting bags. Remember the way little flowers and names were written on cakes, before there were pressurized cans to do it? I bought what resembles a giant icing applicator with a giant nozzle. The pros don't bother with giant icing applicators, they use oversized caulk guns which are refilled by inserting into the bucket and vacuum sucking the goo into the chamber. This caulk gun is expensive and I am not convinced it is necessary. I reconsider and buy the fancy gun anyway after making sure that I can return it if unused.

Since Doug wants to start installing cabinets, sink and countertop, I need to finish the kitchen wall first. (Years afterward, as I contemplate that first attempt, I keep thinking why I couldn't have started somewhere else. Anywhere else.)

I look at the gap between the logs, trying to remember the display at the store. What I am now looking at and what I remember seeing are very different. The gap in display logs is equal along the length of the logs, so that the backer rod slides in nice and tight. The gap along the length of our logs has knots sticking out, unmatched contours, and varies in size by several inches. I can put my fist between the logs in some places and barely a finger in others. This is asking a lot from the backer rod. I cut and shove, cut some more. Finally I have the space filled and am out of backer rod.

With bucket of goo and icing bag in hand, I imagine myself ready. I sacrifice a large serving spoon in order to transfer the goo into the icing bag, which proves to take more hands than Doug and I have between us. Hands that are now all covered in a sticky mess. At least I don't have to worry about the icing bag falling out of my hands. I roll the top over and squeeze. Nothing comes out.

I roll harder and squeeze harder. Nothing. I hand it to Doug. A dribble. At this rate, we will both have carpal tunnel and tendonitis by day's end and nothing to show for it. On to Plan B. Bring out the big gun; lever action, vacuum sucking chink gun that is.

CHINKING GUN

It is downright exciting filling up the chink gun the first time. I take off the nozzle, stick the gun into the bucket and pull back on the plunger. The chink sucks right up into the chamber. I screw on the nozzle tip and pump the trigger along the backer rod between the logs. As I lead the tip along the rod, a perfectly round length of chinking appears. But now what? I have no idea how to spread it out. One by one, I curse my way through our toolbox. Trowels leave gouges, spoons leave concavities. No matter what I use, the goo sticks to the tool. I read the instructions, more thoroughly this time, and find that plain water is the release agent. I re-purpose an old spray bottle, fill it with water and spray it on both the tool and goo before spreading. Voila! But once the chink starts to set up, it's too late to go back and try to smooth it out. The first couple passes look like little whitecaps on the ocean. Right behind where the sink will be.

When we return to Yellowstone that weekend, I describe my traumatic chinking experience to some friends. Linda, a sweet Maryville, Tennessee, volunteer, listens intently. I didn't think any more of our conversation until a few hours later when Linda appears at our door with present in hand. She hands me a spring steel narrow cake icing spatula about 1 ½ inches wide. I hesitated. "It's OK, it's yours now," she says of her contribution. She has really given this some thought. After our next trip to the cabin and back, I can hardly wait to report to Linda that she is beyond brilliant. I continue to use the spatula on every last gap.

As I suspect, our budget and our cabin design are in conflict and don't allow continued use of the commercial closed cell backer rod. The amount we need prods us to look for alternatives. Since our gaps are so irregular, the backer rod isn't always a good solution. One day Doug hands me a large sheet of 2 inch thick Styrofoam. I'm not sure what he is thinking, but he suggests just cutting it to fit the gap. I start playing around with this idea, and after awhile find that I can eyeball a stretch between the logs, cut off a chunk of the Styrofoam and whittle it to a form fit. I get fast and accurate carving foam, only to discover that Styrofoam beads produce a certain amount of static electricity. Some days when I climb down from the ladder, I am coated in tiny white beads.

I complete the interior chinking first before beginning the outside. If I have all the necessary supplies on hand, I can work for hours non-stop. Granted, the only necessary supplies are chink, Styrofoam, a few rags, spray bottle, and Books-on-Tape. Cassette after cassette, book after book this summer, I am working my way through the Livingston Public Library. (Sometimes I practice my evening campfire program that I present as part of my duties as an Interpretive Ranger at the Grant Visitor Center, imagining in my mind each slide as it comes up on the screen before the audience of 500 eager Yellowstone visitors.) I know that once I move outside, being on the ladder will slow progress considerably. I will lay a bead of chink as far as I can stretch my arm on several of the Styrofoam inserts, then go back and smooth them out. Work with one tool then the next. It seems efficient. But on really hot days, the chink starts to form a crust if it is exposed to the sun for too long before being worked. To avoid this, I always work my way around the cabin, keeping in the shade as much as possible.

The crucial test that chinking undergoes is withstanding movement of the logs. Just like a stick-built house settles, so does a log cabin. Only more. The logs continue to shrink in girth, and since our logs were green, not standing dead when they were cut, we have a lengthy period of shrinkage to expect. By the time I finish chinking, more than two years have elapsed since the logs were harvested, but there is still movement. The chinking material is stickier than bubble gum in hair, but it does have limitations.

Warping of logs, walls out of whack, unstable foundations, each one of these can have a domino effect. When I worked at the Snake River Ranger Station in Yellowstone, I would often stare at the log walls of the entrance kiosk and the back-country office. While other employees studied bears or geysers, I might have been the only one thinking about chinking. Call it premonition. I noticed how and wondered why, in several places, the chink separated from the logs. These structures were Lodgepole pine, not Douglas Fir. Was it a function of poor application, poor chink material, settling/warping, the nature of Lodgepole Pine, or something totally otherwise? With each wall I complete in our cabin, I keep a watchful eye for signs of deterioration or potential problems. I just want to confirm that, after my initial stumbles, I've found the right method, the right tools, and the right rhythm.

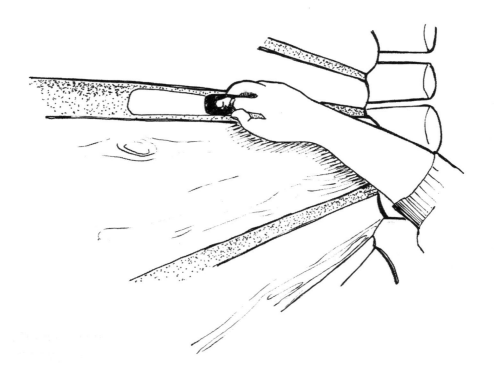

A layer of chink goes on over the styrofoam backer.

Doug

17

MOSTLY, I TALK TO O'MALLEY

One thing is for sure. We have to do something. We have to do the best we know how at the moment...; If it doesn't turn out right, we can modify it as we go along.

--Franklin D. Roosevelt

U pon our arrival back in Montana, we find that summer

has made an appearance and our road has melted out, giving us access by old Rusty. Nancy has made arrangements to begin her new job at Grant, and soon she is gone leaving me and O'Malley alone at the tipi. I have plenty to do and plenty to think about. First, I need to arrange for someone to put on a metal roof; this is not something I'm going to tackle on my own. Also on my agenda this summer are enclosing the gable ends with board and batten, finishing the dormer windows, building a brick hearth and installing two woodstoves. I also need to put in doors and windows, trim around them, build some kitchen cabinets and figure out where and how to create a staircase. My plate is full. Equally full is Nancy's agenda. Her task is to chink the gaps, inside and out, a thankless assignment and a horrible way to spend her summer weekends.

I make some calls to several roofing contractors but they just ask for the calculated square feet and a few other questions and quickly give me a rough, by-the-book estimate. None of them want to take a half a day to come and see the job. One contractor is nice enough to refer me to a guy who used to work for him. Immediately, I call Jeff and he agrees to come for a visit so he can see the obstacles I describe, the 2 track 4WD road, the non-square dimensions, the lack of a driveway to the house site and a generator for electricity.

Jeff follows my convoluted instructions to get to the cabin several days later. I hear him coming about a half a mile off through the forest. O'Malley, as usual, runs down the road to greet him and escort him to the worksite. Jeff crawls up on the roof like a monkey in a tree, measuring and calculating, walking around as if the surface were flat. He gives me a price and I accept then and there. It's a good deal. He needs some money up front to pay for the materials but says I can pay him the day he arrives with the roof panels. Together, we go over the endless list of things I need to do before he can put down the metal. Jeff leaves for the day, but not before he hauls up five or six rolls of roofing felt and tacks them down. Just like that, the cabin is more-or-less weathered in. The OSB (Oriented Strand Board) sheathing is now protected and tools will stay dry unless the rain blows sideways through the gaps in the logs. Jeff has about three jobs before mine and gives me a date in late June when I can expect him. My first order of business is to complete the dormers, which includes getting their walls sheathed and shingled. I also need to get the stovepipes installed and any other protrusions through the roof in place.

I resume my work schedule on the cabin from the previous summer, but now I'm working six days a week with one day reserved for laundry, shopping and mail pickup. Nancy visits on her weekends from Yellowstone, spending all of her time chinking, chinking, chinking.

The cabin with the shingles installed on the dormers and board-and-batten installed on the west-facing gable end. The roofer is due in a day or two.

There is no end to the jobs I have before me. I keep a notebook in my overall's chest pocket and it quickly fills up with lists. General lists of the tasks themselves, the dormers, the doors, the windows. I have small drawings, lists of problems that require solutions, lists of groceries, places to visit, tools needed. I have detailed lists of fasteners and small parts I need. Since there is no shortage of things to do, I tend to shift from one job to another if, say, I run out of nails or some other necessity. A trip to town takes half a day with a minimum of two hours spent at the hardware store and lumberyard, so I make those errands happen in the morning when I am showered, teeth are brushed and I'm not exhausted.

You say, "Showered?". Indeed, we have constructed a rudimentary shower. I have built a small level platform of scrap 2x4s to keep our feet clean. The water bag is overhead, using the old rocket launcher winch to haul the five gallons of water into position. It's situated in a sheltered place, not out of modesty, but because the wind seems to pick up each and every time we stand naked and wet. The water is heated by the sun with our Sunshower brand bag. It's clear on one side and silver and black on the other, the idea being to maximize the solar gain. We put it out in the morning sun and by the end of most cloudless days the water's surprisingly hot, but, of course, on rare gloomy days it's a different story. Sunny days mean a shower and cloudy days mean a damp rag under the armpits.

I'm working harder than I've worked in years, and I have all kinds of thoughts in my head. Because I'm working on the dormers and getting ready for the roofer, I'm spending an inordinate amount of time on the extension ladder which incidentally, is a fine weight loss regimen. I seldom have any free time and when I do try to read a novel, I fall asleep immediately. I am constantly challenged physically and mentally. Each night I pore through the books in my library because I always have another problem to solve. I'm never bored even for a minute and sleep soundly every night, even though I have problems unsolved.

My contact with others is minimal, and I rarely see anyone other than Nancy for two days and nights a week. Mostly, I talk with O'Malley. I find that suddenly I have a lot of tolerance for small-talk with guys who work in the lumberyard and the ladies who are clerks at the hardware store. My summer's going by at breakneck speed, and I don't really have time to think about think about whether I am enjoying my life or not.

Jeff, the roofer, is on my mind. I am forced to take a guess where the two woodstoves are going to be, and do my best to get the thimbles in place and some insulated pipe and a cap on the chimney. Thimbles are metal seats that allow a hot stove pipe to safely exit the roof and provide support at the same time. Their installation requires that I saw two holes in the roof. Cumulatively, I walk several miles back and forth between where the pipes pierce the roof and the interior of the cabin, moving the ladder back and forth as well.

About the time I'm ready for the roofer, he shows up with a pile of metal on a trailer. He's had a devil of a time getting it here on our horrible road. I write him a check and he hands off the green, painted metal flashing that will go where the dormer walls meet the roof. Now I can attach the flashing and put on the shingle siding and be ready for the roof. I help Jeff haul each piece of the metal by hand, 50 yards, from the trailer to the cabin. Next day I am up on the roof putting down flashing. Jeff returns a few days later and puts the metal roof on in three days of scary, slippery work. This is just the second time I've hired someone else to work on this cabin.

I can now bring in the ancient radial arm saw that I have acquired in a trade with my friend Al. It may be old, but nonetheless, allows me to make precise miter cuts and rip boards and will be essential for the interior trim. With the roof on, I can put in windows and doors, and construct cabinets. In fact there is no end to the work we have ahead of us.

In August my entire family arrives for a week of vacation. They have rented the same vacation house about 20 miles away between Bozeman and Livingston on the south side of the Interstate. We have Leslie, Darrell, Sarah, Noah, Andrew and Cooper from Seattle. Then there's Peggy and Tony, Anna, Ellie and Kate from Denver and Amy from Houston. We have old-timers, teenagers and pre-teens. Their plans are to spend about three or four days helping us around the cabin. I have about a dozen laborers to assign whatever tasks I choose. Only my brother-in-law Tony has extensive experience doing any kind of construction related work. Tony, Leslie and I build the framing of the crawl space enclosures. I get Darrell several bundles of cedar shingles, hammer, nails and he's back to his favorite activity; tacking shingles to the crawl space enclosures. He's had plenty of practice on their Rose Cottage and loves the smell of the cedar shingles, the process of snapping chalk lines, selecting just the right shingle to cover the seam and tacking it up. He's doing a very handsome job and he stands back frequently to admire his work.

Taking advantage of our free labor, Nancy organizes several work parties of cousins to gather some rock along the road, pick up pieces of wood and trash from around the cabin, and we get Andrew to build dry rock walls between the piers and under the sill logs. Soon the entire foundation is fully enclosed, the cabin worksite is cleaned up of all residue and I have a large pile of firewood to burn.

I look around and Amy is painting the cabinets a nice crisp white, and Peggy is staining the window trim the same green as the roof. Here and there are gaps in the logs, but Nancy is making remarkable progress on chinking. Not right at this particular moment though; she's driving Rusty, leading the road crew in scavenging rocks from the roadside.

To a person, the whole family is overwhelmed by the changes from last summer. Now the pile of logs is gone and a cabin sits in its place. Walls, roof, porches, the loft; the components are beginning to resemble a home. It is immensely encouraging to have them here and remark on our progress. Darrell, who watched the little Rose Cottage rise from nothing appreciates the work involved and tells me he can't wait to come back for a visit some cold winter and spend a night in the cabin. I agree with him; I can't wait either.

Aunt Leslie and niece Kate, who is all of 8 years old, are brave enough to spend one night with me in the tipi. Strangely, it is on this night we get our first snow of the season. So far this year, only July has lacked snow. It is only an inch or less, and it's all gone by noon but everyone is truly bewildered by the Montana weather. I'm pretty sure Leslie and Kate's memories of that night in the tipi are clearer than mine. They remind me about the dripping tipi poles, the warmth of the fire in the little barrel stove and the mistaken relief in the middle of the night when they heard the rain finally stop, only because it had turned to snow.

Andrew sticks around with me for a week after everyone else leaves. I learn that he's actually worked as a hod carrier on some Seattle construction project. It's the perfect opportunity to build the hearth that the main woodstove will sit upon. He already knows how to mix the "mud" so we make the trip to Bozeman where I have a bunch of used bricks squirreled away. Back at the cabin, I can concentrate on building the hearth while Andrew provides me with masonry cement mixed to the perfect consistency. Unlike the one I built in Manhattan so many years ago, this hearth turns out well, now that I have the proper tools and a little bit more experience.

After I put Andrew on the bus back to Seattle, I pick up the used woodstove from my barn in Bozeman. A friend helps me load and unload it and set it up on the hearth where it looks perfectly appropriate. With the addition of some single wall pipe the stove is ready to use. When a hot fire is burning, the bricks soak up heat and release it into the cabin all night long, a perfect heat sink.

One of the projects I work on during the summer of '96 is the water system, and it turns out to be the most fun and satisfying of all. It has three main components. Part One is the collection system. I install plastic gutters on the north and south sides of the cabin. The south side gutters feed into some 3 inch PVC pipe and take it to the collection point on the north side. On the other side of the cabin the water collects in the gutter and flows straight down into the cistern.

Part Two is the cistern itself, which is an old Snorkel redwood hot tub that will hold 500 gallons, at least. It's sitting solidly on deck blocks and redwood 4x4s. I've covered the tub with a hinged wooden lid and on it sits a water filtration system. The filter is basically composed of a brand new plastic wastebasket, some screen material and eight gallons of sand.

Part Three is the plumbing. At the kitchen sink sits a brand new, old fashioned pitcher pump that will pump water 12 to 15 feet vertically. I run some PVC pipe from the cistern to the sink and hook up the pump. The sink itself is salvaged from a junk pile and is a large white enameled, cast iron two basin variety. It is hooked up to a "French drain", which is a very simple device well known to French farmers. PVC pipe runs from the sink through a P-trap, down through the crawl space where it runs underground, horizontally out from under the north side porch. There, it goes into the French drain, which is a 50 gallon trash can, large holes drilled into the bottom and filled with sand. It has a lid and is buried in the dirt so it's below the frost line. The theory is that the grey water will hit the sand and filter through it to the ground. Food particles and other residue are trapped on top of the sand and common bacteria decomposes the whole mess. Clean water goes into the soil. It's very simple and very efficient and works without problems. Finally, every component is in place. I've tested all the systems by pouring buckets of water in the sink and on the roof and tracking its progress. Now all we need is rain.

Eventually, a few weeks later nature cooperates and we get an afternoon cloudburst. For 15 minutes the skies open up and water flows through the gutters, down the PVC pipes and pours into the old redwood hot tub. In a matter of moments I've captured about 200 gallons of water. I'm outside in the downpour, absolutely enthralled, soaked to the skin, watching every facet of our collection system, running back and forth from south side to north side, down on my knees at times, trying to see where I'm losing water. The hot tub is leaking like a picket fence from the bottom and sides. A rather brownish liquid gushes from the filter as all the finest particles in the sand are washed into the tub and through the cracks onto the ground. It's raining so hard the system is overwhelmed, gutters backed up and overflowing.

But the downpour slows to a steady drizzle for a few minutes while the system catches up and starts working like we planned. Now, the pores of the dry redwood begin to expand and swell. Suddenly, the cistern is more-or-less water tight up to the water line, but I've lost at least a hundred gallons. The filter, having flushed itself out, proceeds to drip totally clean, clear rainwater. As the rain slows to nothing, I run inside to the pitcher pump and start to crank the handle up and down. Nothing gushes forth. I go to the hot tub and scoop about a gallon of water to prime the pump. Eventually, clear, clean rainwater is flowing out of the pump then swirls around in the sink and down the drain. I am absolutely flabbergasted. I simply can't believe everything worked as it was drawn up on paper. Actually, it is just a minor matter of physics. Water flows downhill and then seeks its own level when confined. The suction that the pitcher pump creates moves the water uphill. "Eureka." Just like that our cabin has running water and I'm thrilled beyond words to convey my pleasure.

On the last day of Nancy's work week she shows up around dusk, and before the light fades, she always wants to see everything I've done during the week. Sometimes there are big and exciting changes, like the water system. Sometimes she doesn't notice because I've done something obscure like putting board and batten on the gable end of the house which no one ever looks at. Nonetheless, she always claims it is the high point of her week. And her arrival is always the high point of my week, and O'Malley's too. He hears her vehicle a mile away, listens for a moment and then is gone heading for the road to escort her to the camp.

Slowly the cabin is becoming liveable. But only because it is summer. There are still gaps in between the logs. Nancy is making steady progress chinking but it is slow going. Flies and moths come and go at will. There are kitchen counters but no cabinets yet. We have a sink and water, but our shower depends on the sun shining brightly every day. There are double pane windows in most of the openings, but we have no doors. Every task I complete seemingly begets three mores tasks. I still need to build an interior stairway and an exterior back porch stairway. Then I'll need to construct railings on the porches and stairways, meaning I have to wander through the woods to find suitably sized saplings to cut and peel. Insulation needs to be installed in between the rafters, floor joists and between the studs on the gable walls, then a layer of plastic as a vapor barrier, and finally drywall.

Details, details, details. More to do than I can possibly imagine. I think back to the walls going up one log at a time, and how agonizingly slow that seemed. I draw strength from that time period, and I know that if I just keep plugging away, everything will work out fine, just as it did with the log walls. The innumerable tasks are going well but I am simply overwhelmed by the sheer number, not to mention the mental gymnastics it takes to complete them. I am anything but a well-seasoned building contractor with years of experience tackling these jobs. But then, it's not rocket science either. I just have to think through each problem, many of them complicated by the fact that the cabin itself is not perfectly level, square or plumb. I think back to the cabins we saw in Tennessee that were so overwhelmingly charming, and they were built a little out of square and plumb. So, I take heart and deal with it one day at a time.

One day we take a drive over to Butte, about 120 miles away, to look for some doors. Butte was once the largest city between Minneapolis and Seattle, an empty brag, if you ask me. Nonetheless, Butte has lost a lot of population over the years. The Berkeley Pit, the open pit copper mine, when in operation was eating up neighborhoods like a cancer. The net result is a lot of rescued doors and windows, and thousands of other items salvaged from derelict homes. We find a couple of doors that will suffice, a 15 lite door for the front and a smaller version for the bedroom in the loft. We find nothing suitable for the back door, so I decide I'll have to build one. All in all, it's a very relaxing day off for Nancy and me. We get to see some countryside, peruse some antique shops and have lunch in a restaurant, quite a change from the rest of the summer.

Another buying trip takes us to West Yellowstone, where a fellow named O. B. operates a business repairing travel trailers. He spends summers in "West", and winters somewhere down south, in Arizona. He has a propane/electric refrigerator for sale that he's pulled out of some down-on-it's-luck trailer. We make him a lowball offer and he accepts. The refrigerator spends the remainder of the summer on the back porch where it works just fine, except that occasionally the gas flame blows out in the wind.

The kitchen is beginning to take shape. We are going to have two cookstoves, one burns gas, one burns wood. We have hauled around a 1920s Monarch gas stove for the past 20 years. It's a beautiful antique with dark green and pale green enamel exterior, and we plan to make it operational. The gas company has reworked the jets for us so that it burns propane as opposed to natural gas. Over in Bozeman, in a house about to be torn down, we find an old 1950s wood/electric stove. Apparently there was a time when electricity either hadn't arrived, was on the cusp of arriving, or was so unreliable, a buyer might want to consider a dual fuel range. This stove is white enamel and would look quite stylish in Ward and June Cleaver's house. One half is electric and the other side is wood fired. Mice have long ago eaten the wiring and stolen the insulation, but the wood side works like a champ. We have a steel plate made to replace the electric burners and it's ready to take its place in the kitchen, both as a stove and as a storage cabinet.

I crawl under the cabin and run gas lines to the stove and the refrigerator, which is now inside, and voila, we have a "modern" kitchen. We have running water to the sink and a French drain going out. No more throwing old wash water out to water the plants and feed the mice. On the counter, we have a large drinking water dispenser which holds about 10 gallons of water and a block of ice. We also keep a Katadyn water filter on the counter to filter our captured rainwater for cooking. We have a gas stove that makes our morning coffee, and a refrigerator that keeps the food cold and makes ice for our drinks. Compared to our recent lifestyle of campstove, ice chest and campfire, it's pretty luxurious.

Late in the summer, on one of Nancy's weekends we discover that we have a home that is pretty much liveable. The main thing it's lacking is drywall. Bare studs and rafters still grace the loft walls and the ceilings. I have hung as much drywall as I can by myself, and given that I'm yet unaware of the existence of a thing called a drywall hoist, I declare defeat and vow to bring in a sheetrock hanger and finisher. But that will have to wait.

We have been steadily acquiring cabin furniture in bits and pieces, an easier task than searching through our storage unit for what we already own. But we need a good couch. On a warm day in early October, a furniture store in Bozeman is having a going out of business sale so we make an appearance and find a wonderful deal on a burgundy leather sofa. It takes quite an effort to get it into the cabin but Nancy and I manage. We look around at our work and we are pleased with what we see.. There is much work left to do, but so much has already been done. It's late afternoon and we call it quits for the day. We take a beer out onto the front porch and sit in the Adirondack chairs gazing out at our view of the Absarokas and the Yellowstone Valley.

Unexpectedly, we notice a plume of gray-black smoke rising from down in the valley where we can't see, but where we know Interstate 90 heads up Bozeman Pass. We wonder; a car wreck, a train wreck? What is causing the smoke? We search for the binoculars and scan the valley. Nancy spots a plume of smoke and flame rising behind the hillside in the foreground. It can only be one thing---- it's a dry pine or fir exploding in flame. It's a forest fire. And by all appearances it is growing at a rapid pace and the wind seems to be pushing it up the valley toward our brand new cabin.

East Elevation.

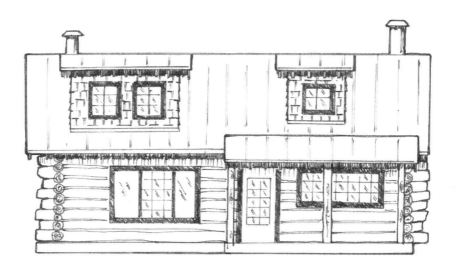

South Elevation

Doug

18

OUR SUBCONSCIOUS HAS SPOKEN

Security is mostly a superstition. It does not exist in nature.... Life is either a daring adventure or nothing.

– Helen Keller, <u>The Open Door</u>

*C*all us stupid, but we don't yet have fire insurance for our

unfinished cabin. It doesn't even have an address. Nancy and I lock the doors, round up O'Malley, jump in the truck and head down the road toward the Interstate and the fire. Our experience with forest fires is not extensive, but we know enough to know we are in a vulnerable spot should the fire advance in our direction. We realize we're not in any great danger of losing our lives, but it is entirely possible we could lose the cabin to this fire if it sweeps up the valley. Nothing we can do, really, other than get ourselves out so no one has to come and save us. Still, the adrenalin is pumping wildly though our veins and I'm driving way too fast. Rusty's bumping erratically down the two-track. Intellectually, we know that we are not in any danger but our nervous systems are not listening.

Down the road about a few miles, we round the bend and we can see flames crawling through the dry grass until they reach a tinder dry tree, whereupon it bursts into flame. It goes up like a Roman candle, in a huge ball of flame, hot pine needles and sparks fill the air above the tree and then settle into the dry grass.

The fire is burning in mixed grassland with some trees here and there and shows no signs of slowing down. The wind is pushing it quickly up the grassy south facing slopes and over the top of the ridge and down the north facing slopes, full of trees. Two or three more drainages and it will reach our cabin.

A few more miles down the road we come upon a roadblock set up by the Park County Sheriff's Office. A deputy tells us that a bad wheel on a freight train has been shooting sparks into the dry grass along the railroad tracks starting inconsequential fires all along the line, but here, the fire has found the right combination of fuel and wind, and it's heading up the drainage.

"You can't go back up the road where you came from," the deputy tells us and we don't want to. We're not that stupid.

"What are your names?" he asks. "And do you know anyone else who lives up there. We're calling everybody we can on the phone and a deputy will be knocking on doors pretty soon."

Unfortunately, we don't have any new information for him. Now the only thing to do is find a good vantage point, pull the truck over and watch the drama unfold.

There are no firefighters on the scene to speak of, other than one fire truck spraying down some embers on the downhill side of the fire. The deputy calls me over and tells me, "Good news, buddy.

The West Yellowstone fire base is sendin' a plane to drop fire retardant. County's got several crews of firefighters on their way right now." This is really good news. So we wait, and wait some more

Finally, the air tanker arrives, we see him off in the distance. The tanker circles, assesses the situation and lines himself up for a drop. Whammo. A huge pink cloud of slime drops from the belly of the airplane and lands on the leading edge of the fire. It circles once more, makes an assessment and heads off for more retardant. He's back again in rather short order and drops another load. Meanwhile, the ground-pounders have arrived and are driving their trucks all over the unburned grass and getting into position. Soon, we can see their bright yellow Nomex shirts and green pants moving up the slope to get in front of the fire, to find a location to begin their defensive actions. I'm beginning to feel relieved. The fire, if not yet contained, will be very soon.

The wildland fire crews are soon all over the fire and we are no longer seeing flames, only smoke. The deputy calls me over again and reports that rain is expected tonight, maybe, but all day tomorrow for sure. Apparently, we're not going to lose our unfinished cabin after all.

We head over the hill to Bozeman. Our renters have moved out so we have had the house back for some time now. The next morning, we wake up to rain and it rains on and off all day. We have dodged a bullet.

During the next few weeks, we settle in to uninspiring jobs to pay the bills and wait for spring. Our lives in Bozeman seem restrained and confined after living in a tipi, working at Yellowstone and traveling all over the United States. We certainly enjoy the comforts of home and proximity to our friends, but winter and working our lousy jobs wear on us. We discuss how we can survive the winter and continue with our seasonal Park Service jobs, which are new and exciting. One Saturday, after six months of re-occupying our house we realize we haven't even unpacked all of our belongings. We still have cardboard boxes sitting here and there, full of books and kitchen equipment. And we haven't hung a single picture on the wall. If actions speak louder than words, our subconscious has spoken. Obviously, our hearts are not into resuming our former lives, and as much as we love Bozeman, we're seeking a change.

In the form of death, change arrives, twice. Within three months of each other, Nancy's father and mother die. Both phone calls from her brother, Jim, come when she is out walking O'Malley early in the morning. It's not that their deaths are so unexpected, as Ed and Sue are in their late 80's. But there was no time for Nancy to say a final goodbye, only to receive the phone call afterward. We drive out to both the funerals in The Region, and return with a few pieces of sentimental furniture, photo albums and dishes. Encapsulating a lifetime's memories into the back of a U-Haul. Nancy is going through a rough patch.

The winter work schedule gives us little time, but we make overnight excursions and spend some long weekends in the unfinished cabin. After we first walk in, it takes at least several hours with two woodstoves blazing to warm it up, but unlike the tipi, once it gets warm, it stays warm. And unlike our house in Bozeman, we are able to keep the entire cabin warm enough to lounge around in our shirtsleeves. No need for sweaters and long-handles.

The snowmobile and trailer makes it easy to get to the cabin. We are slowly learning how to drive the contraption with the trailer attached, and realizing the importance of having a packed base to ride on. As the snow gets deeper over the winter, venturing off the packed base with the trailer attached can be treacherous. The snowmachine can easily get bogged down if the snow is too deep.

We discover a design flaw in the cabin itself. The open loft, with just a knee wall for safety, allows huge amounts of heated air to collect up there. The bedroom has walls and a door and stays comfortably cool, but if anyone were to try to sleep in the open loft they would be, at first too warm and then too cold toward morning. It will be a summertime task to build a wall full of windows to enclose the loft.

Outside on any given morning, we find new tracks of all kinds of critters. Small rodent-like tracks betray the existence of an ermine, the wonderful animal that spends summers as a brown weasel and winters as a snow white ermine. The bears are all in hibernation, but we discover moose tracks, coyote, occasionally deer and elk scat. Some nights it is so very dark the only things visible are stars, and some clear nights, the moon lights up the snowy landscape almost as if it were day. On occasion, when we make trips to the outhouse in the dark with a flashlight, we see green dots in the distance, animals staring back at us and the light reflecting off the rods in their eyes. It's hard to determine just what we are looking at, but O'Malley, who always stands guard on the porch while we do our business, must know. He can see them, his eyes shine exactly the same way when the beam of the flashlight strikes his eyes.

Overall, we find the cabin to be exceptionally comfortable. Still, it is primitive. There are walls and ceilings with exposed insulation between the studs and joists. It is remarkably light and airy during the day with lots of south facing windows. On the plus side, at night we have kerosene lamps and candles that provide a delightful glow to the interior as the light reflects off the golden hue of the log walls. I enjoy looking at the cabin at night from outside, with the cheery yellow light flowing through the windows onto the snow, turning it from blue to gold. Inside, it is supremely quiet. There are no house noises like a refrigerator compressor humming, a furnace blowing warm air or a TV blaring commercials. Outside, no street noises, no hum of traffic, no airplanes overhead. Outside there is no sound whatsoever; the snow soaks up any noise. Inside, there is only the sigh of the fire in the woodstove, or a spirited crackle when I add more wood. Or the sound of O'Malley breathing contentedly in front of the hearth.

Lack of a shower is no problem if we stay for just a few days at a time. Obviously, it's going to be a problem if we spend any amount of time here. It enters our mind that a bath house, with some kind of shower or bathing apparatus would be very civilized. The Lehman Brothers catalog features composting toilets and propane wall lamps, so we begin picturing our lives, living here, with a few more comforts. Our vision of Forest Service or NPS cabins have already gone by the wayside and we start thinking about certain refinements. Our wish list starts to grow: solar electricity, hot showers, a driveway so that we can more easily navigate our way from the road to the cabin site. Where once this cabin was envisioned as a weekend getaway, we now begin to think of it as a place to live all the time.

When we bought our house in Bozeman, it was owned by a couple going through a divorce, one of the reasons we got a good deal on it. We've made substantial improvements to the house. The former owner left dozens of unfinished projects in progress and we have finished them all. Right now, a housing boom is under way in Bozeman and so, we weigh our options. Selling the house would put some cash in our pockets. It would allow us to make some needed improvements on the cabin that just can't be done with out help. We could get a bulldozer up there for a day to cut in a driveway, we could buy some solar panels. It would also leave a fair amount of money in the bank, a cushion against catastrophe.

Over the winter, I learn that I can have my old job back at the South Entrance and I've also been contacted about a new position in Resource Management at Grant Village where Nancy will be returning to her job. Everything is pointing toward rejecting the resumption of our old lives in Bozeman, and continuing our focus on our new lives in the cabin and in Yellowstone.

With some sadness, we put our house on the market in late spring. We think we might be able to get it sold before school starts up in September. But almost immediately, even before we are aware that the house has been shown, we have two offers on the table. Both of them are slightly over our asking price, so our bluff has been called. Suddenly, we've contracted to sell our house, I have a new job and soon we'll have some change in our pockets. And more change in our lives.

Doug

19

A WONDERFUL COLLISION OF IDEAS AND TIMING

A lot of people ask me if I were shipwrecked, and could only have one book, what would it be? I always say, "How to Build a Boat".
– Stephen Wright

Once we sell our house in Bozeman, we are flush with

cash. We pay off the miniscule mortgage on the land and put the rest in the bank. No longer are we operating on a shoestring. Now we can begin thinking about improvements that were impossible without some money behind us. We have three major projects that we'd like to accomplish. One is a driveway, the second is solar electricity and the third is a shower house.

We have been driving right to the door of the cabin for some time. We found a route we call "The Path of Least Resistance" that can be attempted only on dry summer days. Any snow or mud on the ground and we can only walk the last 50 yards, which is not a major problem unless you are carrying groceries or bricks. The Path of Least Resistance begins with a slight hill and then turns into a very steep hill, at the top we have to make a sharp right turn or we'll run right into the tipi. The Path then winds through the forest on a side-hill, along the north side of the ridge to the cabin. The first time I drive it I'm worried that the truck will roll over. It's a feeling that is worse when I am on the lower side of the truck. Somehow, being on the high side is not so freaky. But over time, we get used to it and in reality, rolling over is not very likely, it just feels like it. Going out to the subdivision road from the cabin, we take a left turn near the tipi, drop off the ridge and for a moment it feels like we are in free fall. This little path is definitely not a long term solution.

Besides being scary and dangerous, the Path of Least Resistance has other problems. It's obvious, at least to us, that we'll get the truck stuck someday. And the path that we are using is beginning to create an ugly scar on the landscape. Cargo also gets thrown around; things break and spill, eggs are crushed, cans roll around the bed of the truck, and even O'Malley prefers to get out and walk.

I call up Mr. Ruggles, an excavation contractor, who arrives on a pleasant summer day to look at the possible paths for a driveway. We walk around the property and discuss feasible routes. I take him down into the area where the house logs were cut. It has several drawbacks, among them, it's the longest route, and more relevant, snow piles up and stays there into mid-May. Ruggles and I throw that alternative out. I wonder if it is conceivable to bust a way through the rocky ridge on the south facing slope. I'm worried that it will require dynamite, or an impossibly large bulldozer to do the trick. I also walk Ruggles over to the Path of Least Resistance. He doesn't see it as a likely candidate and refuses to entertain it. That's okay with me.

We agree to the choice of busting through the rocky ridge and then I ask him for a price. I'm worried that the work will come at some exorbitant figure that will physically hurt, but he throws out an estimate of $500 for a half day, if all goes well. I'm so relieved I accept and don't bother to get any more quotes. We agree that he'll do the work on a day I can be there, a week away.

A week later I hear a bulldozer clanking up the road. I hear it from the time he starts it up, takes it off the trailer and heads up the hill, because it takes a half hour for Ruggles to arrive crawling along at a snail's pace. Eventually, I see Ruggles through the trees and he's driving a tiny little yellow critter. I had expected a much larger dozer and I begin to worry if he will be able to chug his way through the rocky ridge. O'Malley and I head out to the site of the new driveway and settle down to watch the show.

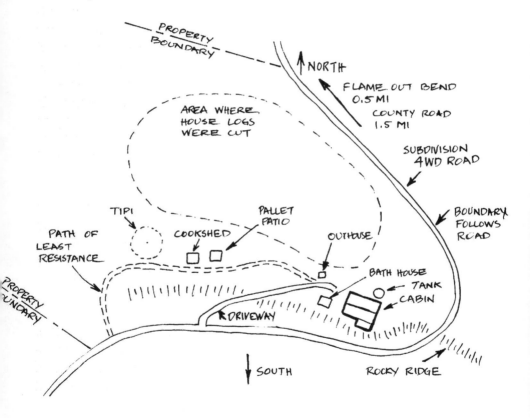

General layout of the east end of the property. Not to scale.

I can watch a bulldozer work most of the day without getting bored and I know I'm not the only one. It appears Ruggles knows exactly what he's doing and he starts by carving out the hillside a little at a time. He moves the dirt over to the subdivision road itself to create a space to maneuver a truck in a 180° turn. An unmistakable smell of wet earth wafts around the work area, mingling with the odor of crushed grass and sage and diesel fumes. The diminutive dozer makes quick work of the few sapling trees that are in the way. Then Ruggles attacks the rocky ridge. The rocks break apart and are shoved aside by the little, well-used bulldozer. I'm crushed and happy at the same time. Crushed because I thought the rocks would put up a bigger fight and that would be exciting to see, but I'm happy that things are going according to plan. But since "all goes well", I can stop worrying that my bulldozer bill will suddenly double. In about three hours, Ruggles has cut in our driveway. He spends a little more time enlarging the turn-around area. In fact Ruggles is through a little before a half day is gone. He asks if I want to use up the extra fifty dollars on a few improvements in the worst places on the subdivision road. He'll spend an extra half hour taking the worst ruts out of the road on the way down. I agree and Ruggles chugs off, but not before telling me I need two or three dump truck loads of gravel on our driveway so that it's not a mud bog in wet weather. But I have a cheaper alternative in mind.

A nearby landowner, who I will call Robert Clanker, has a dump truck and has made me an offer many times. He will bring up a load of crushed concrete that he gets almost free from the local ready-mix outfit. Clanker tells me it's an excellent road base and over time sets up somewhat like what it was in its former life, concrete.

Clanker is a Christian fundamentalist who believes that man was put on this earth to make as many changes as possible, or as many as man desires, or something. I don't quite follow his line of reasoning. Clanker is not a native Montanan. He's from back East somewhere which doesn't stop him from adopting cowboy boots, a western shirt and a beat up cowboy hat, but he's told me he hates horses. I've had a number of discussions with Clanker in which he's revealed to me that he's an anti-environmentalist. He thinks

Yellowstone National Park should be sold to the highest bidder and broken up into luxury home sites. He's figured out that global climate change is a big hoax, there can't possibly be too many people on the earth because they are God's creatures and they wouldn't be here without his blessing, and the animals and trees are there for Clanker's personal use. He don't need no stinkin' permits or no dad-gummed huntin' license, neither. The National Rifle Association is doing God's work and more guns make better Americans.

I know that Clanker would probably have brought his ancient bulldozer up here and charged me a pittance to cut us a driveway, but Robert enjoys recreational bulldozing way too much and it's unlikely he would leave a blade of green grass or a tree standing. Clanker has already recreationally bulldozed all over his own 20 acres several miles down the road. Incidentally, it didn't require a permit for him to make his property a horrible eyesore. Bulldozing is like a lot of other hobbies, you have to know when to stop.

But in the interest of saving money, I hire Clanker to haul up three dump truck loads of his special gravel. Nancy is at the cabin on the day he arrives with the first load. She gives Clanker directions on where I want the gravel unloaded so he backs his dump truck up the new driveway, over the little rise and down into the very un-level parking area. As Clanker commences to dump his load, he unfortunately forgets to unhitch the chain on his tailgate. The dump bed rises, the gravel begins to shift, and Clanker, already on uneven ground, finds the cab of the truck lurching into the air. Nancy sees the cab of the dump truck leave the ground and come slamming down onto the earth again, launching back up and jerking back onto the ground, all the while going backward down the hill like a bucking horse in reverse. Finally Clanker and his dump truck hit a very large fir tree, whereupon the chain breaks and the load of gravel dumps itself on the edge of the forest. Clanker, glad to be alive, tells Nancy he will bring up equipment to rearrange the gravel onto the driveway.

In any case, Clanker's crushed concrete works well enough, and the price is beyond reasonable. I hate to reward Clanker but, in all fairness, he does what he said he would do and I pay him what he is owed as he requests, in cash. So Robert Clanker is probably a tax cheat as well as a "good Christian".

Dealing with the kerosene lamps leads us to buy three propane wall lights from the Lehman Brothers catalog. After I hook them up with copper tubing, we finally have beautiful, bright white light in our cabin. We install one in the kitchen near the sink so that we don't have to leave washing dishes til the morning light. The other two we rig up in the living room so we can have sufficient light for reading. Still, we can find lots of reasons for having electricity. We are without a toaster, for instance. If we want to run a vacuum cleaner, we have to start up the generator. We have a Cuisinart in storage that would be nice to use once in awhile. A VCR and a TV are also in our storage unit and it would be nice to see a movie on occasion. The list goes on and on. Now that we are living in the cabin full time, and not using it as a weekend place as was our original plan, we have changed our minds about a few of our original ideas. Electricity is one of the things we miss the most, and it's one of the things we were sure we could do without.

To bring in electricity is still financially impossible. The nearest buried electric line is about a mile away. The co-op will allow us to amortize our payment of the initial electrification project, but that means a monthly bill, every month, whether we use electricity or not, for a goodly number of years into the future.

But there is another option: solar electricity. We've bought a few things from the Real Goods company, and one day their solar power, wind power, off-the-grid catalog arrives in our mail box. The catalog does a good job of lining out what is needed for off-the-grid homes. They know most people have a very sketchy understanding of solar power and they do their best to define the basics. They also assure us that every situation is totally different and that we need to fill out their form and send it in for a personalized quote for our particular situation.

I begin working on their request for a quotation and so the learning process begins. They need to know our latitude, for solar is a different proposition in the tropics as opposed to the northern latitudes. They ask our general location. Are we in sunny Montana or cloudy Maine? Our yearly hours of sunshine will be calculated for us, along with our expected number of cloudy days given our location. Do we have an alternate energy source, like a generator, or are we on the grid? Additionally, we are required to estimate our daily need for electricity. Will we be running a Mr. Coffee for two hours a day? How much will we use a computer? Do we have a washing machine, a water pump, a stereo, a TV? And more importantly, how many hours will we use each of those appliances each day? There are a lot more questions regarding our particular situation, but I'm sure you understand their line of reasoning.

I send in the form and wait a week or two for my answer. Their quote is rather reasonable, around $3,000. They put together a package containing: three solar panels, a mounting device, a controller and an inverter along with a few incidental items. They also advise me I'm going to spend a few hundred bucks at the hardware store and I'll need four heavy duty, golf cart type batteries. It sounds too good to be true and my main concern is will I be able to do the work myself? I'm a reasonable carpenter, but I'm no electrician. Can I wire a controller and an inverter? I don't know. I get on the cell phone and call my contact at Real Goods. After I describe my situation, Joe asks me a few questions about what tools I own and what I've done in the mechanical arena; have I wired an AC switch, an outlet, have I ever wired up a DC appliance in a car or truck? I say yes, I've done all those, but that's about all. Joe is convinced that I can do it with no external help, save a call to Joe himself, every once in awhile.

We send off a check and in a few weeks packages start arriving in our mailbox. Three boxes containing solar panels arrive one day, and the inverter the next. A couple of days later several more boxes arrive until I have all the components. A set of instructions is enclosed for each component and Joe has provided me with a schematic that is convoluted, but a few phone calls later I have it figured out. I begin a step by step process of installing the system. I order the four batteries and buy the remaining wire, switches, outlets and paraphernalia from my friendly Ace Hardware store.

I set a metal post in concrete, install the panels facing south and at the proper angle, install the inverter and controller and batteries in a ventilated box in an unused area off the bedrooms upstairs. Over the course of a week, Nancy is banished to the crawl space under the floor, running wire and drilling a hole or two though the logs. It's not a pleasant job in January, but somebody's got to do it. She reports that there's evidence of more than a few critters making their homes down under. The slope of the ground under the floor doesn't help, and one corner is so tight Nancy can barely maneuver the drill into position. Outside, on the exterior log wall, I have an on/off switch and a grounding rod pounded into the ground. I wire up about six or eight outlets downstairs, most of them in the corners on the floor. A few other outlets are upstairs, two in the bedroom and two in the loft.

Finally, on a bright and sunny morning, I throw the on/off switch and then run upstairs to look at the controller. It's a device that manages the other components and it has a state-of-the-art digital readout. I punch a button and find out I already have electricity coming in through the panel and the components are charging the batteries. A cloud passes in front of the sun and the input drops to nearly nothing, and then shoots back up again as the cloud passes by. The controller also tells me the condition of the batteries, and about three other factors. In short, everything I need to know to manage our energy usage. In the event we get three or four days with no sun, something that can happen in winter, all we need to do is fire up the generator and plug the controller in, and the batteries charge in an hour or so.

It takes more than one day of sunshine to charge the batteries for the first time, so at the end of the day we run the generator until we have a full charge. That evening we turn on electric lights for their trial run. Oh, how wonderful it is. We turn on more lights than we need and play the stereo just because we can. We plug in the cell phone and charge it up, what fun. From here on out, electricity is essentially free, save the burning of a gallon of gas or two, now and then.

There is quite a learning curve to efficiently operate a solar system, but we have it figured out in about a week. There is no need for me to go over all of the details here, but a few should be interesting. All of the appliances we use are AC, that is, normal household lamps and stereos and the like. Whenever the inverter, which transforms the DC power stored in the 12 volt batteries to AC current, whenever it senses a load such as a light being turned on, it powers up and a small humming noise is heard while it's doing its work. The inverter uses a little energy transforming electricity from DC to AC. We have to find the setting on the controller/inverter that senses a lamp being turned on but not a puny little draw like the cell phone charger. The cell phone will charge up each night as we use electric lights. A small load that you are hardly aware of, for example, the clock on a microwave (not that we have one) can turn on the inverter and keep it on 24 hours a day, wasting the electricity in the batteries. So, if you are going to use a microwave, which generally has a digital clock, your choices are: unplugging it after each use, putting it on a power strip and turning it off after each use, or getting a DC microwave that doesn't involve the inverter at all. DC appliances can be used as long as you wire them up directly from the battery, like a car accessory.

In the winter we need to watch our electricity usage on a daily basis and run the generator once in awhile, like Sunday evening after I've watched a fuzzy, snowy, almost indecipherable football game coming to us free over the airwaves. TVs use a significant amount of energy. In the summer, we hardly need to pay any attention to the solar system at all. We can't even begin to use all the energy we take in. The TV is never on and the sun charges the batteries before 10:00 in the morning replacing the energy we used burning lights the night before. We only need to use the generator when we are using a power tool or the vacuum cleaner.

The availability of electricity allows us to bypass the pitcher pump at the kitchen sink and install an electric water pump. Actually, the pitcher pump remains, the water flows out of it like a faucet when you throw a switch, and it doesn't need priming.

In a wonderful collision of ideas and timing, the water pump sparks an idea. Maybe we can use an electric water pump and a propane-fired, on-demand water heater to build a shower system. We have been in the process of building a small outbuilding to contain a composting toilet and a rudimentary shower, and it is almost finished. We have known for some time it is completely possible to collect water off the roof, and more than we can use. By merely putting gutters on the new bath house, we can collect water and direct it into a tank sitting inside on the concrete floor. A small propane heater, whose original purpose is to provide enough warmth to allow decomposition of human waste to take place in the composting toilet, also makes it possible to store water in the building without it freezing.

Our friends Okey and Karen give us an old claw foot bathtub, and with a little help, we manage to get it into the bath house. I install a French drain, similar to the one handling the waste water in the kitchen sink.

We order a propane fired water heater from Real Goods, after first asking them if an electric pump will be sufficient to force water through the heater, and enough gallons per minute to cause the heater to turn on. They don't see why not. We also order a couple of 100 gallon water tanks. One goes on the floor and one sits in the rafters above the old bathtub. When the water heater arrives, I hang it on the wall and hook it up to propane. I screw the water pump to the wall, run some wires to it, put it on a switch, and begin running water lines. I'm not a plumber, but I have learned enough about plumbing here and there to know how to proceed. It's actually very enjoyable running plastic PVC pipe. Like logs, they are very forgiving. Cut it with a hack saw, smooth the edges, add some primer, then some cement, put the pieces together, and voila, you have a plumbing connection.

I know it seems complex, but it is truly simple indeed. Rain or snow falls on the roof. The heated interior melts the snow and on warmer days, water trickles into the gutters and down into the tank on the floor. Throw a few valves and flick the pump switch and water flows through the water filter and into the upper tank. Light the heater, throw a few valves, turn on the switch and hot water comes out of the shower head, flows over the naked body, and down the French drain. Finally we can have a hot, refreshing, cleansing shower at any time, not just at the end of a sunny day. By turning the switch on and off, we can conserve water and actually take a very nice shower with five gallons of water. On a rainy day, we splurge, and take a seven gallon shower. It absolutely transforms life at our cabin. Our hair is cleaner, for one, and two, we don't wait until it's terrifyingly necessary to take a shower.

The bath house, already boasting a composting toilet and a propane heater now has a shower. It has taken some creative thinking, but solar electricity is the last piece of the puzzle to make a hot cleansing shower possible.

The composting toilet works pretty much as advertised. After each use we add a scoopful of peat moss and rotate the handle, which rotates the drum. Every few weeks we maintain the toilet, and pull out the compost. It has little or no odor and has the appearance of dark garden soil. We throw the contents of the tray onto the snow or onto some grassy area on the forest floor. A composting toilet is certainly not for the squeamish, but it's better than an outhouse, and uses no water at all. Additionally, it's very good for the soil.

Now, we can drive or snowmobile right to the back door and unload our groceries. We enjoy movies on VCR and can flick a switch and have a light come on so we can read a newspaper or book. We can shower any time of day and our toilet is in a heated bath house. All this at a fraction of the cost of our house in Bozeman. Our major improvements are substantially done and for the time being we can relax on the porch and enjoy our cabin. The moment has come that we dreamed about during the construction phase, but is it a good thing?

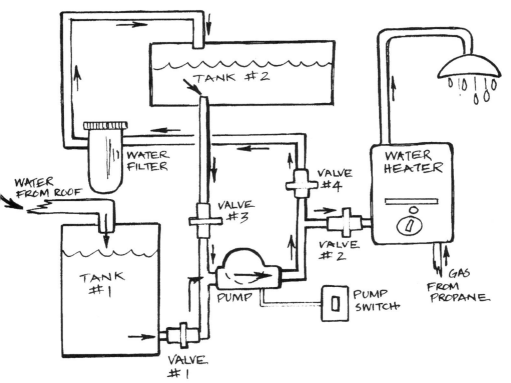

To shower: Open valves #2 and #3, close valves #1 and #4, turn on pump. To fill upper tank: Close valves #2 and #3, open valves #1 and #4, turn on pump.

Doug

20

IF IT GROWS, FLIES, SWIMS OR WALKS

Relegating grizzlies to Alaska is about like relegating happiness to heaven; one may never get there.

--Aldo Leopold, <u>Sand County Almanac</u>

I must be living some kind of charmed life. I have accepted a

job offer from Yellowstone National Park to work in the Resource Management Division. There is no way I can be certain what they find in my background that makes me qualified. Perhaps it is portions of my resume; a B.S. in geography from MSU, or my two seasons working the entry-level position at the South Entrance. More likely it's a combination of factors, the chief one being that Nancy has housing that I can share with her in Grant. I have no illusions about the Park Service in Yellowstone and the strange condition that some jobs are funded, but unless you have housing, there is no job. Housing is very limited in the interior of Yellowstone and the Resource Management Division is allotted last, after Law Enforcement, Maintenance and Interpretation.

At this point, I'm not sure what exactly I'm getting into or what Resource Management does, but I've been assured that I will love it by people who should know. The bottom line is; it's a job, outdoors in Yellowstone; how bad could it be?

This time, "they" are not wrong, I do love it. Resource Management in Yellowstone is charged with, obviously, managing the resources within the boundaries of the Park. That means the wildlife, the plant life and the thermal features, primarily. Our duties include killing exotic weeds to counting spawning cutthroat trout. We spend time in the backcountry, camping out on occasion, or more frequently, using one of the patrol cabins. We conduct surveys of one of the grizzly bear's most important food sources, white bark pine cones, to predict availability and document resulting bear behavior.

Resource Management is responsible for clearing some of the backcountry trails of fallen trees, managing volunteer groups who work on various projects in the park, overseeing the compliance of researchers such as geologists, climatologists and archaeologists, just to name a few disciplines. We respond to all vehicle accidents to assist in traffic control and bio-hazard clean up. I could go on for five more paragraphs detailing what RM does on a daily basis, but the point is, if it grows, flies, swims, walks or erupts, RM tries to manage it in the most natural state possible.

In the southern part of the park, RM also performs part of the duties of the Bear Management office. Managing bears, and other wildlife, is of course everyone's favorite task. In theory and practice, bear and human interactions are almost always a bad thing for the bear. People tend to like to feed bears, which habituates them to humans, making a disastrous backcounty encounter more likely. That is, if bears come to associate people with food, they lose their inhibitions regarding humans and approach campsites, looking for and sometimes finding food. Feeding bears almost always starts bears on a path of destruction. Bear/human encounters, where a bear gets a food reward generally means that a bear will be very dead, very soon.

That's why, anytime bears are spotted near the road a ranger is likely to be there, making sure there are no incidents of feeding. As a veteran of many 'bear jams' I can verify that people do crazy things. They will abandon their cars in the middle of the road, all four doors open, engine running, dog in the back, and mom, dad and the kids all 100 yards off the road taking pictures of a tolerant bear. People will encircle a bear, 50 or a 100 of them, totally surrounding a grazing bear, leaving the animal no path of escape. I've arrived at a bear jam and seen people standing on a cut-bank of a creek watching a bear fishing 10 feet below, and the crowd begins to encroach, trying to get a photo, making it likely that either the bank will collapse or someone will get pushed off the edge, lemming style.

For the most part, I find bear jams a very enjoyable part of my job. It can be hectic, arriving on scene to find traffic blocked and people too close to the bear. Or it can be very relaxing, to arrive on scene and find plenty of safe parking available and the visitors all behaving themselves, keeping their distance, with cameras clicking and binoculars and telescopes being shared and passed around. It is the best time to educate people about bears and I have many interesting conversations. And it is always enjoyable spending an hour or two watching a bear, generally a grizzly, in its natural habitat.

The park was founded, I believe, mainly on the strength of its thermal features. In 1872 there were bears and bison, deer and elk wandering around many places west of the 100th meridian. Now, there is almost no place in the lower 48 where that is the case except Yellowstone and a few other parks. It is ironic that today, people are more fascinated by the animals than the thermal features.

Hardly a day goes by during my 10 seasons in the park that something exciting or unexpected does not happen. Every day is gorgeous, whether it's the view of Yellowstone Lake or a herd of bison wandering through Hayden Valley. Some days I see sights that haven't been seen in Yellowstone in one hundred years; seeing wolves, whether traveling alone or hunting elk in a pack, always fills me with awe. Some days I see things that break my heart, like the cow moose with two broken rear legs, hit by a car and dying by the side of the road. I am forced to shoot her between the eyes. Or watching another elk cow, who in turn is watching its day old calf being killed and eaten by a grizzly. I am filled with frustration and sadness when I come upon six head of elk chased onto the thin ice of the river by wolves, trapped by ice, freezing and drowning at the same time. There is nothing anyone can do, or anything anyone should do.

After eight seasons in RM, I begin to have trouble keeping up with my workmates. I'm limping around with a bad knee, wearing a sling on my right arm from a workplace accident; I've ruptured a biceps tendon trying to move a loaded, chest style freezer from the back of a pickup with three others. My knee won't allow me to participate in some of the daily tasks. I can't walk with a loaded pack nearly as far as I once could. Riding a horse for a full day is agony for the last four hours. I'm in my mid-50s working with kids in their 20s. Something has to give, and it's me. Sadly, my days as a Park Ranger are just about over.

Nancy

21

ORPHANS AND CASTAWAYS

A really companionable and indispensable dog is an accident of nature. You can't get it by breeding for it, and you can't buy it with money. It just happens along.

--E. B. White, <u>The Care and Training of a Dog</u>

Anybody who has ever had to put down a dog will

understand. If you have had to do it more than once, you know it never gets any easier. Dogs love their caretakers unconditionally, so much so they go willingly on that last trip to the vet's office, right into the little room that becomes their death chamber. The vet shaves the foreleg and gives the needed time to say the final goodbye. We know we are seeking reassurance that we are doing the right thing, if you can call it that. Then the vet inserts the needle, and in an instant, our best friend's eyes glaze over and the spark is snuffed out.

We are driving 50 miles to a ranch outside Wilsall, Montana, following up a newspaper ad for a puppy. It is lonely after nearly 12 years as a two-dog family, and now it is nearly a year since we'd spread Cisco's ashes at the cabin site. When old Cisco exhibited difficulty walking the mile and a half, we started leaving him in town when we worked on the cabin. There will always be a part of him up there, we just regret the timing. He watched us pack up tools and head off, and we felt bad not sharing the adventure. The hind leg that once hosted a steel plate gave out, and the other leg from years of overcompensation, had also said "enough". Cisco was our first "child", and after 16 years, it was time to let him go. Pancho, now 12, is always reluctant to mobilize into action and rarely moves off his bed. Sometimes, I put my hand in front of his nose, in hopes of feeling a little puff of breath. We know his days are growing short too. As we drive over the Bridger Mountains and up the Shields Valley this early spring afternoon, my mind is a canine slide show.

Our dogs are members of our family. They do, however, come from humble beginnings, all orphans and castaways. First and foremost, they are mutts. I firmly believe that mutts are far superior to purebred dogs. Their gene pool is obviously larger; they are not so susceptible to skeletal disorders, and their owners are a different breed as well. Additionally, you don't have to take out a bank loan to purchase a mutt. We don't consciously know it, but our only dog-search criteria over the years is a black coat with white chest and white-tipped paws.

I still tear up when I think about Cisco. Doug had surprised me with this tiny ball of Humane Society furry energy for my birthday our first year in Bozeman. When he was six months old, he had escaped from the yard and was hit by a car in front of our house. Maybe the driver never knew, but he never stopped. A neighbor kid found him and ran screaming "Your dog's been hit! Your dog's been hit!" At first, the vet didn't think he would make it through the night since he had been crushed pretty badly. Once stabilized, the vet presented three options to repair his hind leg: remove the leg and leave him a tripod; put the leg in a cast where it would atrophy and drag; or implant a steel plate to bind the smashed bones and remove the plate a year later. As he described the options, we could not imagine Cisco as a tripod or with a nonfunctional leg. We were poor and barely getting by, but without discussion we both blurted out approval to proceed with the steel plate. Cisco recuperated rapidly with his steel leg and only began to experience difficulties much later in life.

Pancho's only resemblance to Cisco is his looks. Their personalities are like night and day. We are in disbelief when people asked "how can you tell them apart?" Cisco had a fire under his butt 24/7 and Pancho keeps a low profile in hopes of escaping all physical exertion. He flies well under the radar. Pancho arrived in our family as a cast-off, dumped out of a car outside our fence. We unwittingly christened him Pancho, the not-so-bright but ever-faithful sidekick of the debonair TV desperado, Cisco Kid. As it turned out, the naming was spot on.

We arrive at the ranch to discover only two puppies remain. The mother is a Husky-German Shepherd cross, and the suspected father is a black lab. One pup is a yellow lab-ish sort, very quiet and not engaged in any usual puppy antics, and the other is black with a white chest bouncing off any surface within reach. There is no question to our choice.

The new puppy sits in my lap on the drive back from Wilsall. Our neighbor, Ron, watches us pull up and funnel the pup into the yard. "What is he, about six months old?" he asks. Well, he's gotten the six part right. He is six weeks. As if an omen, he not only grows into his paws, he outgrows them---fast. If this dog was a kid, the parents would be constantly complaining how he was growing out of his pants and shirts and shoes. I only have collars to worry about. This guy just keeps on growing, all the way to 125 pounds.

We name him O'Malley, in keeping with ethnic monikers. In retrospect, and staying with Spanish, *Diablo* (devil) might be more appropriate. Everyday he grows a little taller and more defiant. I enroll us in a dog obedience class to be held at the local county fairgrounds. At the first session, the instructor announces that if our dog disrupts the class for more than five minutes, we will be asked to retreat to the rear of the field. After spending 40 of the scheduled 45 minutes during the first three classes at the back of the field, O'Malley and I drop the class. O'Malley needs lots and lots of exercise, and I feel if he is tuckered out, he will calm down. The only problem with that theory is that his endurance and stamina increase at a faster pace than mine. He is Olympic quality and I am not. O'Malley is smart; we half jokingly say that O'Malley makes executive decisions. The real joke is on us. If you ask him to do something he doesn't want to do, or at a point in time he does not want to do it, then it is out of the question. He is on his own agenda. There aren't enough hot dogs in the world to change his mind. He doesn't fall for stupid people tricks. Until he is eight or nine years old he is just downright incorrigible.

His appearance is striking and people always inquire about his breed. We begin to identify him as a "German Huskidor", a contraction for a German Shepherd, Husky and Labrador. His

floppy ears are now erect, tail curled, shoulder-high to my hips, and paws the size of a Yellowstone wolf. In a word, he has charisma, and he knows it.

At the cabin, O'Malley experiences new heights of freedom. He patrols his territory, beating a path from tipi to cook shed to outhouse to cabin site, and then expands into the underbrush and trees. Hunting is his passion. It is somewhere in his genes. From the time he is a pup, he practices his skill hunting our gloves. Leather work gloves are his favorite. Set a pair down and one invariably disappears. I imagine a secret leather-lined underground dog-cave. He casually saunters up, all nonchalant, then swoops in and hauls off with a glove in his mouth.

On walks around the cabin property, he chases anything in fur or feathers or slithering on the ground. When world-class sniffing turns up no animals, animal parts suffice. Femurs, rib cages, antlers, skulls, and hides, as long as it is disgusting. Sometimes he carries a bone or antler for miles, other times stealthily burying it. A year later, he can return to that same buried bone or antler and unearth it. He is always on a hunt and never lets his guard down. The front porch of the cabin, elevated over a rock ledge, provides a wide angle lens for stalking. I trust O'Malley's keen senses. When his ears are in hypersensitive mode and his body rigid, I follow his eyes. I know they will be fixated on a chipmunk, squirrel, coyote, deer, elk, moose, bear, or mountain lion, in ascending order of importance.

One summer evening in 1995, we are driving north through Yellowstone in our pickup, Rusty. The speed limit in the park is 45 mph. O'Malley is in the open bed in the back. He has developed the habit of standing on the wheel wells so he can hang his upper body over the side. To complicate matters we forget to unleash him from the frame. Doug luckily gets a glimpse of him going over the side. He is still attached to the leash, running/dragging alongside. Not wanting to stop abruptly and take the chance of thrusting him under the tires, Doug brings Rusty to a stop as quickly as he dares. O'Malley has been on the run of his life. I load him into the cab, wrap him in my jacket, hold him on my lap and start inspecting his paws. They are bleeding where the nails are ground down. It doesn't appear that anything is broken, but we aren't veterinarians. There isn't a vet in Gardiner, so we keep driving the 50 miles to Livingston and call the emergency vet number.

We explain the situation and the vet tells us to leave O'Malley with him and call the next day for an update. When I show up, the poor critter looks like a miniature race horse, bandaged up to his hocks in bright blue wrap. Understandably, the vet is none too pleased with me and instructs me on the proper method of tying a dog in a pickup if it must be there at all.

Later in the fall, Doug and I are no longer able to be on the same work schedule at the South Entrance. Yellowstone is winding up its tourist season and skeleton crews will be closing facilities soon. Doug and I head to the cabin on different days and pass off O'Malley en-route. Yellowstone is mandatory "on-leash" for pets, so O'Malley revels in the new arrangement since he now spends two weekends every week at the cabin. Late one night, as I am sleeping soundly in the tipi, O'Malley bolts out the tipi door. It is nearly a full moon and the illumination outside creates pools of light. O'Malley is stalking back and forth guardedly, growling lowly, then is gone, out of sight. I opt to stay in bed and wait out whatever it is. I have no idea whether to worry or not. A few minutes later, very slowly and majestically, an animal strides directly in front of the tipi door. In the light of the moon, I automatically assume it is a deer from the ruddy coloration. Then logic kicked in, reminding me that deer don't 'walk' that way and they don't have three-foot long tails. Yep, it is a mountain lion. I don't move, I don't breathe. And, much to my surprise, I don't pee in my pants. All it has to do is make one 90 degree turn into the tipi but the lion maintains a straight line. If a pin drops outside, I will hear it. I wait and wait for O'Malley to return. I decide if he tangles with the mountain lion, he is on his own. He will come back if he can. Twenty minutes later, he returns, alone. I hesitate to light the kerosene lamp so I feel him all over for wounds and blood. He is clean, panting heavily from his outing. I resume my sleep, fitfully. O'Malley keeps watch.

O'Malley is developing a reputation. Not that we really keep a tally, but every time he has a flirtation with near disaster, we figure that another of the "nine lives of O'Malley" just got used up. The following summer, I am out jogging on our two-track road near the cabin. I see a glimpse of brown/black on a bend in the road ahead of me, followed by three smaller flashes, all heading down a ravine. There is nothing else it can be---a black bear sow and three cubs. O'Malley is already in pursuit, bypassing the road and charging down the ravine. Even though, intellectually, I know it will do no good, I yell for him to come. Branches break, growling and yipping pierce the morning quiet. All at once, O'Malley is airborne, flying up the ravine and landing on the road. Then, and only then, he decides to come to me. In fact, he roars right past me and doesn't stop until he reaches the cabin. I occasionally look back to see if his sparring partners are following as I also high-tail it up the road. Arriving well after O'Malley, between gasps of air, I tell Doug what had happened. We bring him into the cabin to inspect him for wounds. Within a few seconds, there is an overpowering odor inside---the smell of bear saliva. Along O'Malley's back is a whitish gooey substance. Under the goo are several puncture wounds.

Spring is calving season in Yellowstone when bison, elk, moose, and deer are birthing. It is a tenuous time. The mothers are fearful and defensive, attempting to protect their little ones from predators until they can run with the herd. Cow elk will hide their calves in a safe place and cautiously graze a distance away, but if anyone or thing crosses the line between she and her calf all hell breaks loose. O'Malley and I enter that zone one evening. I walk him on his leash in Grant Village along the service road accessing the employee housing area. An oncoming pickup truck starts honking and swerving. My first reaction is that the driver is drunk, coming from the employee pub, a not so uncommon sight. The honking grows more emphatic, and I realize the driver is trying to get my attention. He is waving his hands and pointing. I turn around just in time to encounter a cow elk standing on her hind legs. My reflexes don't kick in quickly enough, and her front hooves clip O'Malley and flatten him to the ground. I tighten my hold on the leash and drag him across the road, the cow elk following in hot pursuit. The cow elk skids on the wet pavement, and I run across to the opposite side. By this time the pickup has stopped and the driver is yelling, "Jump in!" "My dog's bloody" I yell in reply. "Jump in!!" he yells more emphatically. O'Malley and I make it to the driver side of the pickup with the elk on our tail and we play a cat-and-mouse game to get to the passenger side and finally get in. My white knight in Toyota armor floors it down the road and the cow elk charges after us. My heart is thumping audibly. I'm almost afraid to tell this latest tale to Doug.

There is a second bear encounter and a second mountain lion encounter. Outings with O'Malley are a thrill a minute. I am mesmerized observing his reactions to wild animals, in that nano-second before the chase. His focus is intense, an unbreakable spell. When he returns, always empty-mouthed, I wonder at what moment he decides to give up, that he knows he can't win. Maybe there is some sort of truce reached in the animal kingdom, an agreement of respect between predator and prey or predator and predator. Or, maybe it is only play-fighting between certain species, and they quit when they are tired. He resumes his hunting perch on the front porch, the slate wiped clean.

There is no better match for O'Malley than life at the tipi and cabin. There are few restrictions or regulations. Except when it is time to round him up to go into town. Then he keeps a safe distance, escapes all attempts at corralling, or plays hide-and-seek until we give up. We drop the tailgate and wait. And wait. Eventually, in his own good time and holding his head high, he strides over and leaps into the back end.

On one winter Sunday, we snowmobile down to the car to head into town. O'Malley runs alongside as usual, and as common, refuses to kennel up when we get to the truck. We've played this game before. We drive down the county road a little ways and try again. This time we wait around a bend a quarter mile or so away, but after 10 minutes there is no O'Malley. Another 10 minutes and still no O'Malley. We turn around, then see the poor dog staggering slowly down the road, not running like before. A red trail follows behind him. He is now very willing to load into the truck. He has a hole in his side and frozen caked blood around it. The young vet tech on duty that Sunday gives him a shot, cleans him up and asks us what happened. The consensus is that he probably got in a dog fight and ended up with a wound. We leave the vet's office with meds and a follow-up appointment in a week. Within a few days the wound starts healing nicely, but his personality changes dramatically. Loud noises easily startle him, he won't jump into the back of the pickup, and he cowers when we enters the room. I want a more obedient dog, but this behavior is suspicious.

I describe this erratic behavior to the vet during the follow-up and they take X-rays, which reveal an indistinguishable object next to his spine. He isn't certain, the vet concludes, but he has a hunch it is a bullet. I am in disbelief. How and when did that happen? The vet admitted that he just isn't sure, and suggests I take the X-rays to the local sporting goods store. The clerks gather round and diagnose my dog's predicament as a 44 magnum bullet, a rather large projectile, lodged at the top of his spine. An entrance wound with no exit. The vet chooses a course of no action; surgery can potentially sever too many nerve endings. The bullet remains, but with help from some medication, scar tissue forms around it and O'Malley recovers and resumes his usual rapscallion behavior. No doubt he sacrificed a couple more of his nine lives.

In the end, it isn't bear or lions or bullets that does him in. It is good old muscular-skeletal problems. And old age. All the millions of leaps off the cabin porch, all the vaults over fallen logs, even the jumps into the back of the pickup, come at a hefty price. At some point he tore a cruciate ligament that went unnoticed for a year. By the time we recognize the problem and schedule surgery, he is probably too old. He now has to use a ramp to climb up the three steps into the house.

The surgery buys him a couple years, but they aren't great years. He's lost his spunk, his drive. His spirit is fading. Our last summer at the cabin is also O'Malley's. His pill box is complicated, and I am fooling myself to think it makes a difference. His breathing is labored and most of his food regurgitated. The weather is record-breaking heat this summer, several days over 100 degrees in Livingston. It is even reaching the high 90's at the cabin. The ground is brittle under our feet. Rattlesnakes hiss out the back door, a new sound foreign to our ears. Another sound in the distance, also foreign to our ears, is that of bulldozers carving out roads to yet-to-be-built houses. Spruce bud worm has infested the Douglas Fir trees, ravaging all new growth by defoliation, and encasing entire limbs in tents or webs. When the sun backlights a tree, thousands of bud worms hangs by strands from branches, ready to plop on unsuspecting passersby. It is gruesome. Our world is spinning. The times they are changing. And those changes lead to tough decisions we have to make the summer of 2006.

Nancy

22

STRANGE TIMES MAKE FOR STRANGE BEDFELLOWS

One can be a brother only in something. Where there is no tie that binds men, men are not united but merely lined up.

– Antoine de Saint-Exupery

*I*t is ironic how an emotionally charged issue can unite polar opposites in an odd alliance. The sixty residents of Lost Springs subdivision are suddenly reaching out to one another in just such an unlikely alignment. The rallying cry is the very real threat of coal-bed methane development, right beneath our homes. What makes this threat more treacherous is knowing that the coal-bed methane drilling would all be done legally, no matter how destructive, as we property owners helplessly stand by.

Tonight, for the first time, many of the sixty land owners will be gathering at a neighbor's house to discuss a plan of action. A fair number of these folks I have never met, but easily recognize their vehicles in passing on the county road and acknowledge with the customary Montana two-finger wave. Some live out of state, waiting to build until retirement, and will not be attending. A few I have had run-in's with over winter access issues or road blockage. And a few are even friends. But, tonight, we are one.

When Doug and I, as well as all the other property owners, purchased acreage in Lost Springs, we bought the rights to the surface land only. The ownership of what lies beneath the surface, the mineral rights, belongs to someone else. Few, if any of us, were the least bit concerned at the time we signed closing papers. What of value could possibly lie below these steep gumbo-laden hillsides?

Split estates, as the division of surface and sub-surface property ownership is called in the West, is common on deeds. A little history helps explain how it became so common. The Homestead Act of 1862 sought to open development in the West by promising 160 acres of land to those that constructed a 12 by 14 foot building and lived in it for five years. They owned not only the surface, but beneath the surface. But by 1910, the government recognized that the surface land was valuable for agriculture, and the sub-surface was potentially valuable for its minerals. So, split estates were created, and the government either retained all the mineral rights or sold them off on their own. Somewhere along the line, the J.M. Huber Co. of Denver purchased mineral rights in Gallatin and Park Counties, underlying some of the most expensive homes in Bridger Canyon and the scrappiest homes in Lost Springs. It is a law that has long over-stayed its welcome, needs radical revision, and is definitely making an impact on us.

We pull into the parking lot at Natalie's "grain-bin" architecturally-designed house on the lower road. I make the distinction of houses on the lower road versus upper road, only because the lower road is plowed by the county, and these homes have all the usual amenities of civilization. Upper road houses, depending upon how much you are willing to spend, have variations of amenities. Natalie is a fashion photographer, her website advertising global, on-location shoots. Once we step inside, it's easy to understand why she offered to host this event; her home is gorgeous. In the middle of the grand, open and airy lower room, other residents are already hovering around the large table spread with finger foods and beverages. The room rises up, flanked by two catwalk levels where I assume the bedrooms and bathrooms are. At the far end of the house is Natalie's studio, which I am dying to see, but now is not the time to ask.

A small core group of residents has already contacted every landowner by phone, email or snail mail with a detailed description of J.M. Huber's impending actions, and a Landowner Petition to write and file a zoning regulation with the county. It's a slow process, but eventually successful. One landowner works in Antarctica, one lives in Germany. A huge percentage are on board, and we feel the momentum to forge ahead. Grinding out the details of the document, making sure not to step on too many toes in the process, it has been a lesson in diplomacy. Tonight's meeting is the final sign-off before submitting it to the Park County Clerk and Recorder.

As I make a point to mingle, something that doesn't come easy for me, I also try not to avoid those with whom I have had conflicts. Lance and his wife Susan are turning from the refreshment table, and I audibly gulp. Pre-judging before we even greet, I am quick to notice he is wearing his trademark black "pleather" jacket. His skin is translucent, his hair platinum, a color of unknown origin. I try to tell myself to focus on the present, the reason why we are gathered, not the past. Instead, I keep thinking about our contentious relationship. I'm sure he's thinking the same thing.

Lance's parcel is on the very, very top, No. 1. Our first encounter with him, which set the stage, was on an exploratory drive up to the top of the ridge with Doug's sister and her husband. We followed an old two-track, not knowing where it led. By the time we got out of the truck to take in the view, we heard a vehicle revving up toward us. An angry ball of halo hair stormed at us, yelling "Is this your land? Do you pay taxes up here?" "As a matter of fact, I do," Doug answered.

In order to transport Lance's doublewide, no, excuse me, "modular home", to his house site, a bulldozer had to widen and straighten the road for a mile and a half. He also expended a huge sum of money to have electricity brought to his doorstep. His turnoff is about a mile from our place. Too bad he chose the cheapest and steepest route, had no gravel laid down and had no water bars cut. Within one season, the road returned to two ruts. In winter, he mounts a small plow onto his pickup, and starts plowing from his double-wide after each snowfall. His plowing piles up a huge amount of snow at our turnoff, and makes snowmobiling over it difficult, and we also have to dig it out long after the rest of the snow melts in the spring. We are furious, and make our fury known.

Lance is a very private person, which I can respect. He wants no one, in no uncertain terms, to step a foot onto his property. One afternoon we are at the base of the hill in our truck and we recognize one of Lance's dogs running down the road. Since we are heading up the road anyway, we decide to drop him off on the way, a short detour. As we start up Lance's turnoff, incessant barking begins. Staked out at intervals on both sides of the road are several hounds, alerting the household to any apparent danger. Lance shoots out of the house demanding justification for our presence. He doesn't seem the least bit relieved at seeing his dog, and we suddenly feel guilty leaving the poor pup there.

I smile, shake hands with Lance, comment that we're doing a good thing, fighting the good fight, blah, blah, blah. I know we are both itching to move on. I say hello to Susan, and for the life of me wonder why she is with him. I know I will never know. Spencer and Pam have just arrived and I excuse myself. Spencer is a former Army Ranger, a fine painter, making a living as an insulation salesman. Pam is a woodworker, crafting her trade for a cabinet builder. They are good friends, inviting us over for Friday-night pizza and a movie. Pam and I have been working together a lot on the zoning document. They are two of the earliest residents in Lost Springs and have seen lots of changes over the years. Spencer is the first person we met after purchasing our property, when he abruptly appeared out of the trees at our camp one evening while out hiking. He was in full camo regalia and caught me off guard. After awhile, I came to realize that is just Spencer. He came up out of curiosity, just to see who the new oddballs are in the tipi. Over the years he and Pam have done a lot of improvements on their property, developed their spring and built a pond with a great stone bridge. They generously allow us to fill our drinking water container whenever we want.

The signatures on the zoning document are piling up as people come and go. Some hang around for quite a time. It's easy to see that many of us don't do a lot of socializing. With the emails and snail mails already received, we have the required number to pass muster to submit to the county. Now it just needs to be reviewed and approved. Closer and closer. Whether this document would stand up in a court of law and prevent J.M. Huber from entering our property and drilling is a bridge we hope we never cross.

Someone introduces us to the folks who just bought the parcel across the road from us. They seem a far cry from the last owner, Barney. I'm not sure if Barney defaulted on his payments, ended up in jail, or is off on some self-guided mission, but we are sure glad he is out of there. A triangular-shaped area of closely-spaced four foot tall stumps is the only legacy he left on the property. Whatever he intended to do with the stumps is beyond me. Barney interrupted our weekends with the noise of him tearing around on his four-wheeler, stopping long enough to fire off several hundred rounds of ammunition. This lasted for several months, then one day he was gone, never to return.

David is there, and everyone asks him how his renovation is going. It's hard to talk to him without thinking of the previous owner of his property. Kevin lived there with his partner Jeri, both of them youngsters from somewhere in the Midwest. They had an on-again, off-again relationship. Kevin was a sweet, quiet guy who came to Montana to live his dream, not unlike many of the rest of us. But it seemed that everything that Kevin touched broke; car, snowmobile, relationship. He always put on a good front, but underneath I think he was a troubled soul. After they split up and moved away, we heard that he committed suicide by hanging himself in Jeri's house, and perhaps we should have seen it coming. I don't know what happened to Jeri.

I think about old Charlie Story, the original resident of Lost Springs. He's gone, moved to Billings to be near family. He lived on the lower road, but I don't think anyone appreciated his double-wide being there. It was cobbled together, a shed roof here, a lean-to there, Charlie wasn't big on aesthetics. But he had a heart of gold. It's true, his place was an eyesore, and he got a lot of flack from more affluent residents who felt he just didn't fit in. But since when does the last resident to arrive get to say, "I don't like it, and I don't want to look at it?"

The times they are a-changing, Charlie. And strange times make for strange bedfellows.

Doug

23

INTRUSION INTO SOLITUDE

All progress is precarious, and the solution of one problem brings us face to face with another problem. – Martin Luther King, Jr.

In 1999 I am offered a springtime position with the Park Service in Moab, Utah. I arrive in Moab around the first of March where it is sunny and bright and the red rocks appear even redder against the brilliant blue sky. The temperatures at night drip into the high 20s and the days, generally sunny and warm are up into the 50s. There is no snow on the ground and none in sight, save the snow visible on the slopes of the La Sal Mountains. It is a drastic change from Montana where snow has been sitting on the ground for several months.

A little earlier on, Nancy had accepted an eight-week long position in Canyon Village in Yellowstone. The winter season is already underway when she reports for duty in Canyon, so she's picked up in a Park Service snowcat, a winter-converted van designed to ride over-the-snow. The only instructions are to pack whatever she needs for eight weeks, including clothes, food, and all incidentals.

My situation is totally different than Nancy's, who is living in Park Service housing, staring out the window at a six foot berm of snow that continually slides off the metal roof of the building affectionately known as "The Dog Pound". When I left for Moab, O'Malley became her roommate at Canyon. It sounds easy, but it requires Nancy to make a thirty-five mile snowmobile ride to Mammoth, and return with O'Malley riding in a kennel on a sled with the temperature hovering at zero. She takes him out four times a day, a run before work, a walk after work, and pee breaks at lunch and bed time. The morning run is always cold, sometimes dropping to thirty-five below, but O'Malley thrives.

I'm able to find a nice apartment in Moab, near the center of town with a roof top deck where I can bask in the glorious sunshine, whereas Nancy sometimes goes days without seeing her shadow. I can walk to bars and restaurants, even to a groovy grocery store. Nancy must drive for an hour on a snowmobile to Mammoth, get in her car and drive to the grocery store in Gardiner and then reverse her path. My night time low temperature in Moab equals her daytime high in Canyon.

We talk on the phone every couple of days and I tell her about my job and the wonderful weather in Moab. She suggests that I use some of my three day weekends to look at a house to buy, someplace we can spend winters in the future. We discuss her isolation and boredom in Canyon. She's introduced to her co-workers in Canyon, but winter in Yellowstone means that everyone wears balaclavas under snowmobile helmets. Outdoors, in subzero temperatures, it's crazy to remove face protection, so she begins to recognize people by voice alone. It takes awhile to put faces and voices together at infrequent social gatherings. Nancy tells me on the phone, she's counting the days until the road is cleared of snow, and her job comes to an end. She's looking forward to joining me in Moab where she can relax in the warm sunshine until mid-May when our Yellowstone jobs begin again.

Truth be told, we are growing a little weary of our life in the cabin. We are conflicted. It is not that we don't enjoy our time there, we do, but we feel a little confined. We have turned an empty plot of land into an absolutely beautiful place to live with a lot of the comforts most Americans expect from their daily life. It is a colossal pleasure to wake up every morning, build a fire, brew coffee and watch the sun come up over the ridge off to the east. If the ridge was a little lower, or the cabin a little higher, I could see the Crazy Mountains from my window. I sit by the woodstove most winter mornings, drinking my hot mug of coffee, watching for wildlife on the slopes of the hillsides, looking for tracks in the fresh overnight snow and tend the fire to take the chill off the cabin. I wait to turn the radio on until I hear Nancy stirring in the bedroom up above.

Silence is broken only by the crackling of the fire. Sometimes the wood smoke is visible from my window, blowing upward and eastward in the gentle breeze. Sometimes it blows sideways off to the south which generally means a storm is coming. Most days I can't see it because it is rising straight into the clear, windless morning sky. The satisfaction we feel living in a building we have built from scratch is enormous.

My days of long hiking and skiing are pretty much over because of my knee, but Nancy continues to enjoy these activities right out our back door. O'Malley is grateful and is her constant companion on regular outings, summer and winter. Sometimes, they are absent for hours, and I just hope that if anything happens, one of them will have the good sense to let me know.

For other diversions, we have books, newspapers and magazines to read. Entertainment is not lacking; we can watch a movie on tape, and we get three fuzzy television channels. We have hot showers all year and running water in the summer. Splitting wood and hauling water from town takes up some of our time, and it's a fair trade; we'd rather do that as opposed to working for wages. Wood is free; natural gas is expensive. Generally, I enjoy splitting wood; it's good exercise. Laundry is an inconvenience, taking it to town, but we haven't yet figured out how to deal with the huge demand a washing machine would place on our water supply and electrical system. Staying busy is no problem, we have projects we work on, small improvements still to make the cabin a better place to live.

We maintain ties with our friends in Bozeman, and Livingston, and we have numerous overnight and weekend visitors, mostly in the winter. They either ski into the cabin along the road, or I snowmobile down and pick them up, hauling everything and everyone up in the trailer in several trips. When we have visitors, we spend the weekend skiing, sledding, cooking and drinking wine, playing board games in the evening. Lonely, we are not.

When we were building the cabin and there was never enough time in the day, I used to dream of the moment I could sit on the porch in the afternoon, look out across the Absarokas, drink a cold beer and have nothing at all to do, no project to worry about, nothing to feel guilty about not doing. That time has come, and after awhile, I don't like it at all. I have little at all to occupy my time, other than reading and splitting wood. We have nothing to fire our imaginations. It's not that we are unhappy with our lives, we're just unchallenged. To satisfy our need for a project, we buy a house in Livingston one October and fix it up and sell it before we head back to work another season in Yellowstone. It's not particularly rewarding, financially or otherwise, in fact it's quite risky so we don't attempt it again.

One fall, on a whim while on a hiking trip in the canyon country near Moab, we decide to spend a day looking at a few houses. One fixer-upper stands out in our in our minds but we can't agree on what to do. We spend the entire drive from Moab to Livingston, arguing and fighting about whether it's a good idea, a good price, a good plan. Back at the cabin we finally agree to buy the house. It essentially gives us a gargantuan project; over time, turning a beat up old house with grounds like a moonscape, into a property with a nightly rental, a shop, two cottages and lush landscaping. Over time our life shifts to Moab while our cabin becomes a summertime retreat.

The cabin becomes our summertime home and even then, it's weekends only. It is a respite from Yellowstone. Some folks think we are crazy needing a break from the Park, but summers are hectic with visitation hovering around 3.4 million people. Our yearly schedule evolves; we arrive back in Montana in May, about the same time our seasonal work in the park begins, and we leave in late October, when the subdivision road becomes questionable and the heat in Moab abates.

While our cabin is our sanctuary, there have also been some intrusions into our solitude these past few years. A young fellow has bought the piece of property next to us and is building himself a home from salvaged materials. He's started out with a corrugated metal grain storage silo. He's doing a fantastic job, a very creative job, and he's a really nice guy, and we're very sympathetic to his labors, but it is hard to contemplate having a neighbor so close by.

On the other hand, rumors have been circulating around the subdivision that one particular neighbor, who is so private that it borders on perversity, is cooking up illegal substances. He certainly has a perfect place for it and it does not surprise us in the least. NO TRESPASSING signs are posted here and there, big chains seal off his road and guard dogs are staked out near his house to sound the alarm. Daily, he patrols his acreage as well as the empty lots nearby. He makes a trip to town every day, seemingly with nothing and returns with nothing.

We know other landowners within our hearing and within our viewshed are working on plans to build some time in the future.

We've heard the clank of a bulldozer now and again, dozing a flat space out of the hillside, knocking down trees that will never be house logs. We've seen buildings, instant rustic castles, being built down on the county road. Houses where the owner flies in from the coast to see how the architect and custom builder are coming along. Houses that use cranes to put logs in place, not home-made skyhooks and rocket launchers. Houses that have three bathrooms inside, and a well that costs $20,000 for the first glass of well water. They are not within our direct line of sight, but make no mistake, the valley is filling up.

Doug

24

SOME PEOPLE CAN LIVE IN A DOUBLE-WIDE BY THE INTERSTATE

He looks into his Dixie cup and looks back up as if surprised at what he found there. The future, maybe.
--Wallace Stegner

"**W**hy on earth would you think of selling?" It's not exactly a question you expect to hear from your real estate agent, someone usually so anxious to get their hands on piece of property. Instead, we respond with questions of our own. "What kind of person would buy a cabin with this kind of access? Without a well?" But Veronica is very complimentary, "The view is to die for." Our real-estate agent, Veronica, is intrigued at the invitation for dinner and arrives with her husband, Tom. The invitation is written on the back of a sketch with driving instruction to the cabin. We sit down to drinks on the deck and the setting sun. No surprise to us, they find the place totally beguiling. Veronica can point out a little clearing, probably 20 miles away as the crow flies, where she and Tom used to own a cabin on the slopes of the Absarokas.

We don't answer Veronica's opening question because there is no easy answer. Our reasons are like the wind, they come from many directions, and sometimes can be strong or mild. Fear of future development, fear of forest fire, not the same without O'Malley, need a new project, no longer hiking or skiing, these are just a few of the why rationalizations circling around in our heads. In reality, it might be that it was the journey rather than the destination that captivated us. I think we know that it is time to move on. Friends and family thought us a few screws loose when we embarked on this project, but now to walk away? A new project beckons, looms just over the horizon. We just haven't defined it yet. One door closes and another one opens.

We take a tour of the various features, Veronica snapping pictures at every stop. I point out the switch near the sink that when toggled, brings water gushing forth from the red cast iron pitcher pump. We proudly show off the 1920s Monarch gas stove and the funky wood/electric/no longer electric stove. They find the bedroom charming, even with the solar components box hidden behind a three paneled dressing curtain. But it is the solar system that is bewitching. I explain the units, the functions and describe what each one does and how they all work together to produce absolutely free electricity. Everyone has heard of solar electricity but relatively few have experienced it first hand. The thought of never again paying an electric or gas bill is enticing. I take them out to the north side and show them the water tank, the gutters, the filter and the plumbing that takes rainwater to the sink. The bath house alone takes half an hour to explain. Veronica and Tom marvel at the shower system, and I obligingly light the heater and turn on the shower for 30 seconds until steaming water sprays out of the shower head. They run their hands though the spray of hot water and feel the softness of the rainwater. Taking a walk around, I point out the corner stakes and show them a plat describing the legal boundaries of the land.

We talk about the new zoning district which prohibits coal-bed methane drilling, in theory anyway. It hasn't been tested for its legal strength.

After our tour, we settle down in the Adirondack chairs on the deck, and over delicious dinner and a nice wine, we discuss the intangibles. The cabin itself is so nicely situated in the grove of Douglas Firs, a cool breeze blows through the open doors and windows while we talk. Veronica comments on the lack of bugs. There are no mosquitoes up here and there never have been. A few flies, maybe, but no mosquitoes.

A few days later Veronica calls and tells us she's busy working on a marketing plan, doing her homework on what kind of money it might bring on the market. And then Veronica says, "Tom and I have talked about buying it for the last two days, ever since we said 'Goodbye' after dinner. We've agreed to come to a final decision when we get together this evening. I'll call you tomorrow morning." Nancy and I discuss this development, is it bullshit? Some kind of ploy? We finally decide that as up-front and straight forward as Veronica is, it's the truth and we are flattered.

Veronica calls the next day and we set up a meeting in town. She says she and Tom decided that they love the cabin but all things considered, it's not the right time for them to make a big investment. At our meeting, we discuss price and talk about marketing strategy. Veronica says the internet is the way to go. There is no doubt in her mind, this cabin will be someone's dream, however, they may be living in New York or Texas, not Montana. Photos she took the other night will turn up buyers from all over the country. But the difficulty is the horrible road and the highly unusual utilities. The cabin has "curb appeal" that rates 11 on a scale of 10. Her advertising will give very few clues as to the location so we won't have yahoos driving around the subdivision. She resolves to talk with each prospective buyer on the phone, screen them for financial soundness, advise them of the circumstances, and if they want to see the cabin, they will have to consent to Veronica escorting them from Livingston.

The price she tosses out to us seems surrealistically high. Or maybe it's not high enough. About two weeks later, Veronica calls and tells us she's been spending all her time on the phone fielding calls from Montana and all over the nation. Several people are making trips from afar to see the place. She'll be bringing a couple by in a few days. "Will you be there? Can you explain the water systems, the solar, the shower?" If she wants us to, we will. Two days later, we hear Veronica's truck coming up the road right on time. She's brought us a couple that, judging by their accents, have come from the southeastern U.S., maybe Kentucky, maybe Arkansas. We can't tell.

They are impressed with the cabin, they like the solitude and the view, but they are nervous about bears making off with one or two of their children, and they wonder if we get snow very often. We're incredulous, but they flabbergast us with another question, "Where is the nearest school bus stop?" Nancy and I have absolutely no idea, but we think it's probably where the county road meets the interstate, about seven miles away as the crow flies. Bears, black bears, are definitely roaming around but they probably won't haul off the kids, and no shit, it snows here in the winter. The three questions make us realize these are not the buyers. This deal will not come to pass.

Over the next month we endure some very peculiar folks and we begin to wonder about ourselves. Are we like these strange people? No, it can't be, we're normal, we think. One day some exceedingly clever individuals put together some clues from the listing on the website, and maybe from a conversation with Veronica, and pull up into our driveway uninvited. We watch them drive by three or four times. They are in a sedan, low slung, 2WD, automatic transmission, how did they even get here? Where this cabin is perched, no one can drive by without our knowing about it and we've been laughing at the preposterous sight for ten minutes now.

"Is this the cabin that's for sale? Could we look at it?" they yell at me from the car as I step out the door onto the porch. As much as I'd like to show the cabin, these folks have irked me and set me on edge. I resent the way they have yelled at me even before introducing themselves.

"We show it by appointment only. Call Veronica in Livingston. Don't come back up here without her." I growl at them. They back up the driveway, not seeing anyplace safe to turn around, and I wonder how in the hell they will get the car up Flame Out Bend. Maybe the trunk is filled with rocks. It better be. In any case, they don't come wandering back on foot, looking for help, and we don't find their rusting hulk of a car abandoned on the road on our next trip out. All must have gone well.

Within the next few days, Veronica brings by two groups that seem like winners. One is a young couple from Bozeman, and Nancy and I can easily imagine them living in this cabin. One glance at the view from the deck and they are hooked. It's easy to look in their eyes and see what they are thinking. They are guileless and transparent, anyone can read the meaning in their gaze; we are living their dream in what they already see as their cabin. They are speechless for a moment, overjoyed that almost everything in the cabin is included in the sale. Chairs, pots, pans, some tools. However, I can easily imagine them happily living here with only a mattress and a camp chair, haunting the garage sales in Livingston and Bozeman, looking for treasures.

The other couple are closer to our age, from Washington State. It looks like they have their shit together. They ask the right questions and seem to harbor no illusions regarding the difficulty of living remotely and off-the-grid. They also seem to project an aura of capability, having been there and done that, and this too is their dream. We don't quite sense the same level of enthusiasm as we did from the younger couple. But we can see these people are quietly enamored of the property too. They're savvy enough to keep a lid on their display of affection. Their questions are knowledgeable, not clueless. Our hopes are high for one of these couples to make an offer.

It is heartening to know there are people who have just as much appreciation for the lush forest surrounding a one-of-a-kind cabin, who are not deterred by the despicable road and the solitude. Veronica said there would be people like this, who would see the beauty in the land and the hand-built cabin, and regard the drawbacks as challenges, not deal-breakers. Some people can live in a double-wide by the Interstate, and some people don't see themselves like that. Veronica said that these people would find us, and so they have.

We get a call from Veronica a day or two later and we have a full price offer on the table from the first young couple. Veronica tells us that this couple didn't pass the economic screening, but they begged and begged to see the cabin. Financing has yet to be worked out and may take some time. Older more financially secure family members are going to need to step up to the plate and an additional visit may be required. We're getting ready to leave for Moab. Our rental season begins soon, and we have no other offers. We'd really love to see this couple have the cabin. Knowing that someone who so obviously loves the place, who so desperately want it, and that they are the kind of kids who, if they can't buy our cabin might just build one exactly like it, it makes us feel better about leaving this place that we have put our heart and soul into, so we agree to their proposal.

A couple of days later Veronica calls and we find out we have another offer from the Washington couple, this one nearly full price. Our hope is that we don't need it, but life is uncertain, so we accept their back up offer and pack our bags for Moab.

Nancy

25

TONIGHT WE REST, FOR TOMORROW IS A WORK DAY

Man cannot discover new oceans unless he has the courage to lose sight of the shore.

– Andre Gide

Monsieur Jean-Pierre Dumont is a wiry little man, a tightly wound bundle of nervous twitches. His movements remind me of a hummingbird, limbs in continuous flight. The papers on his desk are in evenly-spaced stacks, as if snapped-to with a chalk line. But this doesn't stop him from fidgeting with each pile, shuffling and precisely replacing paperwork, appearing to be searching for a missing object. His obsessive-compulsive behavior is freaking me out, and I just want this paper-signing over before I chicken out.

Doug and I glance at each other, trying desperately not to roll our eyes.

M. Dumont is said to speak no English, and I confess, I never hear him speak a word. He is the *Notaire*, part title investigator, part clerk and recorder, part assessor, part lawyer, mostly God, and all fluttery. We are dependent upon Helene, our French real estate agent. She is half French, half British, a very handy combination during this real estate transaction in southwest France. Her French is fluent, but even Helene has difficulty getting a word in once M. Dumont begins talking at a speed equivalent to his body movements. Now he is both painful to listen to and watch. The French are huge on pomp, and at any moment while M. Dumont ceremoniously reads the *Attestation*, the sale document, I half expect a drum roll or trumpet salute in the background.

In the year since we sold the cabin, the question, "What next?" is always in our thoughts and conversations. How can we possibly top that adventure? The proceeds of the sale were promptly tucked away in a hard-to-reach account, waiting for a serious decision.

We ponder buying another property somewhere in Montana, Utah, Colorado, or New Mexico, and spend weeks poring over maps, driving back roads to towns we hope are yet undiscovered. What we discover is that everybody is now into buying fixer-uppers, and few bargains remain. We are adamant about buying a house with "good bones", something we'll fall in love with. As we index through the possibility of renovation projects, we also start thinking about another passion, traveling.

Ever since 1987, when Doug and I pedaled our bicycles 3000 miles around Europe, we have longed to return to France, Italy and Ireland. The hill towns of Italy and France, with narrow, cobbled winding streets, hooked us big time. We couldn't get enough and have the photos to prove it, with brightly colored doors, shutters, brass door knockers, postage stamp gardens, village *boulangerie/panetteria*, and the cheese, wine and bread. Little by little, an idea surfaces. Why not buy a fixer-upper in France or

Italy? Ireland is out of contention as far as Doug is concerned. He remembers day after day of cycling in pouring rain. No wonder Ireland is so green.

A quick search on the internet reveals an assortment of books about buying property in France and Italy, although most of them are written for a British audience. We begin to study the ins and outs of the legalities of owning property as an American. One archaic law in Italy drives us over the border into France. A property owner has absolutely no authority to ask a tenant to move---ever!

Some years back, we had spent time in Provence at a house belonging to friends of Doug's sister. Our days were consumed by morning vegetable markets, village-wide *marche de puces* (flea markets) or sipping *cafe au lait* or wine (depending upon the time of day) on tiny outdoor tables. We rented a canal boat and cruised up the Canal du Midi for a week, sleeping on board and stopping in small villages to re-supply. It was a far cry from the suburban, franchise happy, typical American town.

Now we are making plans for a scouting trip to France. Twenty years ago, in '87, we cycled through Normandy, Brittany and into the Loire. We have been doing some homework, looking at relative property values, hours of sunshine, population density, things that on paper seem to make sense. But, as anyone who has ever bought a house knows, you've just gotta go there and see for yourself. We line up a house trade with a French couple in Provence. It gives us a good starting point. As a real eye-opener, we walk into an *immobilier's* office in a charming Provencal village and suggest looking at some houses in the area. She pleasantly inquires about price range. We tell her the figure for which we sold the cabin, and her smile disappears. The apartment she shows us, if one could call it that, situated above a fast-food restaurant, is one large room with a sink but no bathroom. Our rudimentary French precludes me asking, "How does one justify this as an apartment without a bathroom?" Provence was way too bloody rich for our pocketbook.

Next on our list, we head to the Dordogne. The countryside is gorgeous, lush with vegetation, unlike Provence. It is early in the season, yet things are bustling. Millions of tourists have found their way to the region as well as thousands of new immigrants, retirees from Britain. It seems crowded and we miss the "Big Sky" feeling of the Rocky Mountains.

We head for another region we feel might be promising about an hour north of the Spanish border, in the Ariege department, due north of the tiny country of Andorra. The Ariege is one of the least populated, least-affluent regions of France, a poor-man's Provence. At one time, towns in the Ariege were famous for their textile mills, an industry long since sent overseas. The Pyrenees form the southern border, wild snow-covered peaks with a number of ski stations high up around timberline. In the summer, rolling hills of huge yellow sunflowers span the horizon for mile after mile. It is rich agricultural land; silage corn, cattle, vineyards, even tobacco. We start to relax, park along the side of the road to take it all in, and know we have found our new home. Best of all, it is sparsely populated and is mostly undiscovered by tourists.

Our time on this scouting trip has run out, but we are successful in identifying the area where we want to buy a house. We stay a few days at a bed and breakfast in a tiny village, and over morning conversation with Alan and Eileen, a British couple, we compare notes. They are close to purchasing an old village house right around the corner. We make plans to stay in email contact and learn from their experience. Several months later, we rent their newly purchased house for several weeks and we vow not to depart until a "*comprimis de vente*", a promise to sell, has been signed. We loosely target a fifty-mile radius of our home base, and spend dawn to dusk viewing houses. Some are rubble, resembling Hadrian's Wall, the pile of stones separating England and Scotland. Some would not be out of place in a sprawling American subdivision.

We have accumulated a dossier of documents for M. Dumont, required for signing the closing papers on our new, 200 year old house. We've opened a bank account, and transferred the right of surviving beneficiary. Under French law, joint tenancy does not exist as in the United States. So, even though the house is in both our names, if Doug were to die, I would be in line to succeed him only after his three sisters and their children. It's not that I don't love Doug's family, but I just felt this might be carrying it a little too far.

For several hundred Euros, we procure an additional document securing Madame N. Procter first in line. I hope I don't have to test the authenticity of the document any time soon. There appears to be no Paperwork Reduction Act in France, evidenced by the certificates and credentials we are obliged to produce. Birth certificates, marriage licenses, divorce decree (me), bank statements, utility statements, health insurance confirmation, everything but my kindergarten roster. I keep waiting for M. Dumont to summon my dossier, which I have neatly contained in a file folder, but he doesn't ask for any of it. Ah, welcome to France. Drum roll, please.

With the precision of a surgeon, papers are rotated counter-clockwise from Doug to me for signing. As quickly as I complete my signature, M. Dumont whisks them away, turns each over and separates them into piles. Helene rapidly informs us of what we are attaching our names to, and like children, we believe her. After what seems like several hours, but in truth only one has passed, we are done. M. Dumont carefully grasps each parcel of papers and places it in a pre-assigned, snapped-to position on his desk. Helene stands to indicate it is time to depart, graciously thanks him, tells us when to expect our copy in *La Poste*, and hands us a set of keys.

Out on the street, I begin to babble all my pent-up questions to Helene. Jet lag has really set in. Yesterday at this time we hadn't yet landed in Toulouse. Last night we stayed at the same bed and breakfast in the same tiny village where we were first introduced to the Ariege. Now we can call it "our village". The house we find is just down the street from Alan and Eileen, where we rented only a few months earlier. We walked right by it every day for a couple weeks, unaware it was for sale. It's three stories and needs minimal work on the first floor, some work on the second floor, but the third floor is an empty canvas. It's on a narrow street sandwiched between two other village houses. The old stone walls have been standing for several centuries but the kitchen is fairly new. Once we see it we look no further. Exposed stone, lime plaster, two hundred year old beams, new tools, new building techniques, a new language. We're pretty sure we found a project.

Tonight we will take it easy. Tomorrow is a work day.

GLOSSARY

As far as I'm concerned, if something is so complicated that you can't explain it in ten seconds, then it's probably not worth knowing anyway.

-- Bill Watterson, Calvin and Hobbes

Board-and-batten	Vertical siding of wide boards with cracks covered by narrow strips of wood.
Chalk line	String loaded with chalk, when stretched and snapped, makes a line.
Chinking	The filling between logs; mortar, mud and straw mixture, or foam and latex.
Concrete	Aggregate of cement, sand, gravel and water, generally steel reinforced.
Course of logs	Logs at one level, enough to encircle the perimeter of the cabin.
Dado	A groove made by a saw, router or chisel sized to accept another piece of wood.
Dimension lumber	Wood milled to standard sizes used in construction
Drawknife	A two-handed shaving knife which is pulled, or drawn toward the user to remove material.
Eaves	Overhangs of the roof.
Flashing	Sheet metal, often bent into an "L" shape, used under shingles and siding to prevent water penetration.

Floor joists	Beams on which a sub-floor is laid.
Footing	Wide masonry support in the ground on which foundation is built.
Gable	The triangular wall space enclosed by the roof at the ends of the structure.
Joist	Support upon which ceiling is hung or flooring is laid.
Kerf	A groove made by a cutting tool such as a saw.
Knee-wall	A short interior wall between the rafters and the floor.
Lag screw	Large screw with a bolt head, used in wood.
Loft	Space upstairs under the roof, with the roof structure as a ceiling.
Notching	Cutting away pieces of wood to allow one beam or log to fit tightly to another.
OSB	Oriented Strand Board, 4x8' engineered lumber in varying thicknesses. Manufactured using flakes of wood and glue in specific orientations. Often used to sheath studs in wood frame construction.
Pier	A horizontal support, usually sits on a footer, can be masonry, concrete or wood.
Plumb bob	A string with a pointed weight attached, used for defining an exact horizontal.
Rabbet	A groove in wood, such as a saw kerf or a router kerf, usually to inset another piece of wood.

Rafters	Beams set at an angle from the top of the wall to the ridge on which roofing is attached.
Shingle	A thin piece of wood, such as cedar, used to cover a roof or less frequently, a wall.
Sills	Heavy base logs upon which other members rest, such as walls and joists.
Spike	A large, heavy nail.
Tongue-and-groove	Lumber milled with a spline on one edge and a groove on the other. They fit together to form a weather tight joint.

Top Twelve Tips for Building Your Own Log Cabin

1. <u>Do</u> buy any tools you will use a lot. You can always sell them when you are done.

2. <u>Do</u> take lots of pictures - you will cherish them.

3. <u>Do</u> take the time to keep a journal, however tired you are at the end of the day.

4. <u>Don't</u> assume building a log cabin is a highly technical endeavor. It used to be done with little more than a plumb bob, ax and horse. You can do it with a chain saw, sledge hammer and a truck.

5. <u>Don't</u> assume that you can't do it just because you lack the experience. It is possible to learn by doing.

6. <u>Do</u>, on the other hand, take the time to gain relevant experience where possible. Attend a log cabin building school for their short or long course for hands-on experience.

7. <u>Don't</u> scrimp on your piece of land – you can change everything but the land.

8. <u>Don't</u> let anyone tell you that you are crazy or that you can't do it.

9. <u>Do</u> your research, talk to your reference librarian and read lots of books about building a log cabin.

10. <u>Do</u> visit as many log cabins as you can, old and new. Visit National Parks with historic structures, log cabin builders and timber frame contractors. Inquire if a National Forest near you has old patrol cabins for rent.

11. <u>Do</u> search the internet for any blogs or websites related to log cabin building.

12. <u>Don't</u> do it alone.

NANCY & DOUG MEET
CORPORATE WORK

PARK RANGERS
LAND PURCHASE
93 — TIPI — OUT HOUSE
94   CABIN CONSTRUCTION BEGIN
95) LOGGING BEGINS
)- ROAD TRIP
96) FAMILY VISITS
97   OCCUPY CABIN ?
         SELL BOZEMAN HOUSE
98   DRIVEWAY ? ELECTRICITY ?
99   MOAB JOB
2000
01
02
03
04
05
06   CABIN SELLS ?
07   FRENCH HOUSE
08
09
10
11
12

Made in the USA
Lexington, KY
12 June 2012